A Year of Jewish Cooking

L–R: Natanya, Lisa and Merelyn.

Monday
Morning
Cooking
Club

A Year of Jewish Cooking

Recipes we can't live without

Lisa Goldberg
Merelyn Chalmers
Natanya Eskin

Photography by Alan Benson

SIMON &
SCHUSTER

New York · Amsterdam/Antwerp · London · Toronto · Sydney/Melbourne · New Delhi

Contents

The Monday Morning Cooking Club Sisterhood 6
Introduction 9
Kitchen Notes 13

Shabbat 17

Sunday Bagels 51

Rosh Hashanah 79

Sukkot + Harvest 109

Chanukah, Purim, Tu Bishvat 143

Pesach 163

Shavuot 195

Shiva + Comfort 217

Recipe Acknowledgements 242
Index 245
Thanks 253

The Monday Morning Cooking Club Sisterhood

Lisa Goldberg
MMCC's 'Chief Pot Stirrer' is, simply, a food-obsessed home cook. Lisa grew up in Melbourne, studied and practised law and, after moving to Sydney for love and starting a family, realised she preferred food courts to judicial courts.

Swapping legal briefs for wooden spoons, Lisa put her heart and soul into our cookbooks, celebrating food, family and community. Along the way, she has created a special and connected virtual communal kitchen on social media. In 2023, Lisa created the YouTube series *Walking up an Appetite*, exuberantly eating, walking and talking her way across Sydney.

Lisa is also a dedicated advocate for our community, using words and videos to share her thoughts on life's serious (and not-so-serious) moments. Lisa lives in Sydney with husband Danny, occasionally feeds their four adult kids and partners, and proudly answers to 'Bubi' from her grandchildren. You'll find her on socials – mid-bite, mid-recipe, or mid-conversation.

Merelyn Chalmers
For Merelyn, growing up with Holocaust survivor parents, food was always the language of love. Grinding poppy seeds in a cast-iron mill, shelling walnuts and making pastry from scratch were essential lessons learnt and are still treasured memories of time spent with her Hungarian mum.

As a public relations consultant specialising in food and wine, Merelyn soaked up the Sydney food scene and engaged with some of the best chefs in town. But there is nothing she enjoys more than home cooking and spending a day in the kitchen perfecting recipes with her MMCC sisters. Her clear communication and pedantic respect for the written word are central to our book creation process.

Merelyn's children have now left the nest and – joyously – the family has expanded. She loves when they phone home for their favourite recipes and relishes hijacking the kitchen when visiting her granddaughter on the other side of the world.

L–R: Merelyn, Lisa and Natanya.

Natanya Eskin

Natanya has always found joy in the kitchen – cooking and baking for family and friends is where she feels most at home. A love of food, especially sweet recipes, was shaped by her Russian grandmother, a wonderful cook whose greatest happiness was found in feeding her family well, and a mother who always baked rather than bought.

Natanya was born and bred in Sydney. While raising her family, food was always the focus and highlight of every Jewish festival. Now that her three children are grown up, she is excited to see them cook for themselves, carrying on family traditions in their own unique ways.

Recently, Natanya returned to another of her long-held passions, teaching. She works as a specialist primary school teacher, supporting children in their learning. She is thrilled to write this cookbook, which combines her love of food and education, to introduce Jewish festival recipes and traditions to the next generation.

Introduction

Our sisterhood started in 2006 to tell the story of our community through food. We wanted to preserve recipes from the past generation for ours, and from our generation for the future. Over many years we have collected, curated and shared hundreds of recipes and stories from our Jewish community in Sydney, then Australia, and then across the world.

As we travelled and talked to cooks, it became abundantly clear that nurturing friends and family with food is the language of love for so many Jewish people. No matter where we live, there are the universal questions: what are you making for *shabbat* dinner; can I have your honey cake recipe; what is the best way to plait your *challah*? We live in different places yet feel deeply connected through our shared values in life, the traditions we maintain and the food we *fress* (eat with abandon).

Our four cookbooks can be found on so many kitchen counters and we are honoured to be part of people's everyday lives. We're overjoyed that our books have become a trusted resource for traditional dishes and have encouraged cooks to create their own family traditions with recipes from other people and other places.

When we started out, our kids were just kids. Before we knew it, they were all grown up. Now they phone home, asking for the recipes of their memories, the recipes that are soaked with tradition, the recipes that have guided their Jewish life. They might not cook them every week, but this is the food they can't live without.

Over yet another cup of tea, we realised we needed just one more book, a guide book for the next generation. It was time to secure the continuity of the Jewish kitchen. It was time for an overview of the main Jewish festivals, their stories and traditions. It was time to ensure the Jewish community would remain connected, to each other and to the past. It was time for this book.

We are a people linked by language, religion and traditions, with ancestry that can be traced to ancient Israel. The Jewish people have identified this way for thousands of years, whether or not we are practising, lapsed or somewhere in between. Jewish communities fall into three broad and sometimes overlapping groups based on their movement across the globe: Ashkenazi (central or eastern European), Sephardi (generally speaking, the Iberian Peninsula, Spain, Portugal; as well as India, Iraq and Iran/Persia) and Mizrachi (the Middle East). These days, Jewish food is generally classified as Ashkenazi or Sephardi.

Much of this book reflects our own Ashkenazi roots but we all love a deep dive into other, sometimes more exotic, Jewish kitchens. Join us in our modern Jewish kitchen, built on heritage, identity and love. Our mission is to create a food legacy and a home that revolves around the kitchen table, with all its stories and banter. We hope this book fortifies generations of tradition in a relevant, modern way.

For those of you who are not part of the Jewish community, this book answers the questions you've asked for many years about our food and traditions. Why do we eat honey on *Rosh Hashanah*? What is the significance of *matzo*? We are so happy to welcome you to our table and share the collective wisdom of the generations who have come before us.

In this book we have new recipes and old. Over the years of cooking the earlier recipes, we've made changes that work for our families, suit our kitchens and are streamlined – where possible – for the busyness of life. Some have been replicated, some tweaked, some changed, and others used for inspiration.

We adore the stories from our previous books, which give us a glimpse into the kitchens and lives of our cooks. In this book, however, we've decided to focus on the recipes and traditions; the stories and original recipes can be found in earlier books for your reading pleasure. Our hearts are full of gratitude and love for the generous cooks upon whose shoulders we stand. See page 242 for the provenance of the recipes in this book.

Ultimately, this book is a collection of must-have recipes to lead us all through the Jewish year of cooking; recipes that need to be shared, recipes that weave and adapt to the needs and demands of a modern kitchen while at the same time nod to our very special traditions.

As always, with love from our kitchens to yours,

Lisa, Merelyn and Natanya
Monday Morning Cooking Club
xxx

Kitchen Notes

We have tested and retested these recipes to make sure they can be replicated in your kitchen. We suggest you read these notes before you start.

On Dietary Requirements and Keeping Kosher

Many in our community follow the specific Jewish dietary laws of *kashrut* (keeping kosher), which includes the total separation of meat and dairy products. Our recipes are suitable for the kosher kitchen.

For more info on dietary requirements, including which recipes are dairy free, gluten free and KLP (kosher for Passover), see the complete list at mondaymorningcookingclub.com.au.

Measurements

We use standard Australian metric measurements.

For cake, biscuit and pastry recipes, precision is essential and we recommend weighing ingredients using a digital scale.

1 cup = 250 ml = 8½ fl oz
1 tablespoon = 20 ml = ¾ fl oz = 4 teaspoons
1 teaspoon = 5 ml = ⅛ fl oz

If you are using a U.S. (non-metric) 15 ml tablespoon, add an extra teaspoon for each tablespoon specified.

Ovens + Kitchen Equipment

Our recipes are tested in a domestic oven on conventional (not fan-forced) heat settings. Ovens can vary and you may need to adjust the cooking time or temperature accordingly. Generally, if using fan-forced (which works well for roasting), reduce the cooking temperature by 20°C (68°F).

To beat using an electric mixer means to use the paddle attachment or K beater.

To whisk using an electric mixer means to use the whisk attachment.

To knead using an electric mixer means to use the dough hook.

A handheld mixer can be used for any beating and whisking.

Lining tins or trays: Grease the surfaces lightly with butter, oil or cooking spray and press baking paper, cut to size, onto the surfaces.

Cake tins: Measured by the diameter of the base. If your baking tins have no markings, write the measurement on the base with a permanent marker.

Ingredient Notes

Butter: We use unsalted butter for cooking to better control the saltiness of the dish. If you have only salted butter, adjust the salt listed in the recipe.

1 stick of butter = 113.5 g = 8 (U.S.) tablespoons = 4 oz

Cinnamon sugar: For coarse cinnamon sugar, combine 2 teaspoons ground cinnamon with 1 cup (220 g/8 oz) white sugar. For fine cinnamon sugar, use caster (superfine) sugar.

Melting chocolate: To use the microwave, put the chocolate (broken into pieces or chopped) in a heatproof bowl, and heat on a medium power, checking and stirring at 30-second intervals to avoid burning. If there are still a few bits of unmelted chocolate left, stir until melted rather than cooking longer in the microwave.

To melt on the stove, use the double boiler method. Bring a small saucepan with about 2.5 cm (1 in) of water to the boil. Place the chocolate in a heatproof bowl that will fit snugly on top of the saucepan without touching the water. Turn the water down to a simmer, place the bowl on top of the saucepan and allow the chocolate to melt, stirring from time to time.

Eggs: We use large free-range eggs with a minimum weight of 60 g (2 oz) in a 700 g (one dozen) carton.

Some recipes in this book contain raw eggs. Always use the freshest eggs for these recipes. If you are at increased risk of the effects of salmonella poisoning, and for food to be served to children, the elderly or pregnant women, please consult your medical professional before eating. It is recommended that any dish containing raw eggs be stored in the fridge below 5°C (41°F) and consumed within 24 hours.

Flour: We mostly use three types of flour: bread (high-protein plain), plain (all-purpose) and self-raising (self-rising).

You can substitute plain flour for bread flour.

You can substitute cake flour for plain flour when making cakes, biscuits and pastry.

To make self-raising flour, sift 2 teaspoons baking powder with 150 g (1 cup/5⅓ oz) plain flour.

Herbs: A handful of fresh herbs, such as flat-leaf parsley, mint or coriander, is approximately 1 loosely packed cup of leaves or half a large bunch. A small bunch of chives weighs around 30 g (1 oz), about ¾ cup chopped.

Lemons: 1 lemon, juiced = 50 ml (2½ tablespoons) juice

Oil: When a recipe calls for oil, use any unflavoured oil such as grapeseed, canola or light olive. We have specified which recipes call for extra-virgin olive oil.

Schmaltz (rendered chicken fat): Collect 500 g (1 lb 2 oz) raw chicken fat. When you cook chicken, collect and place any raw fat (a little excess skin is ok) in the freezer (or ask your butcher). Chop the fat and skin and put in a saucepan with 1 cup (250 ml) water. Bring to the boil over high heat, then reduce the heat to medium-low and simmer, uncovered and stirring from time to time, for 45 minutes or until the bits of skin start to brown. Continue to simmer until the skin is crisp.

For extra flavour, you can add ½ onion, roughly chopped, for the last 10 minutes of cooking time.

Strain through a fine colander into a heatproof jug. Allow to cool and then refrigerate for up to one week, or freeze in small portions, ready to use in your *Matzo* Balls (page 169), Chopped Liver (page 25), *Cholent* (page 42) and Potato Kugel (page 95). Depending on the skin vs fat ratio, this will render around ¾ cup *schmaltz*.

(If you want to go all the way, and really step back in time, add salt to the fried skin and onion to make *gribenes*, an old-world topping. Delicious on *challah*).

Salt and pepper: We use two types of salt: fine or medium-grained, best-quality salt for most cooking and baking needs and flaky salt for seasoning after cooking.

All salt measurements in this book use fine-grained salt. If you are using flaky salt, double the volume needed. The weight remains the same.

If you use kosher meat, it is salted as part of the koshering process and needs less salt added during cooking.

We find it useful (for recipes where pepper is measured) to grind a handful of black peppercorns with a spice or coffee grinder every few weeks and store in a jar in the pantry.

Shallots: Shallots = spring onions = green onions = scallions

French shallots = eschallots

Sugar: We bake with caster (superfine) sugar. You can substitute with white (granulated) sugar but in baking recipes that call for creaming butter and sugar, you will need to beat for longer.

We use icing sugar mixture when a recipe calls for icing (confectioner's) sugar.

Yeast: We use instant dried yeast or dry yeast.

1 sachet (envelope) dry yeast = 7 g = 2¼ teaspoons = 14 g fresh yeast

KITCHEN NOTES

CHAPTER ONE

Shabbat

FRIDAY NIGHT, SATURDAY LUNCH

Saturday is *Shabbat*, our sabbath. It is often considered a day of rest, of spiritual immersion or prayer for some and of family time or football for others. In this busy world, *Shabbat* offers the opportunity to disconnect from the everyday.

Like all festivals in the Jewish lunar calendar, this day starts the evening before. *Erev* (the eve of) *Shabbat* begins at sunset on Friday with candle lighting followed by blessings over wine and *challah*. We light two candles to honour the two commandments (*mitzvot*) of remembering and observing the Sabbath.

Friday night's '*Shabbas* dinner' is a cornerstone of our community, the essence of so many of our traditions. It is the reason many of us learnt to cook, with lessons from mothers, mothers-in-law and friends. Before we knew it, we'd mastered the essentials for our own family table.

Growing up, this was the dinner we were never allowed to miss. Now, for the three of us, it is the coming together of all the generations. It is the most precious time of the week to bask in the sheer joy of family. For some, particularly people who have made new lives in Australia from other places, it is the coming together of friends as chosen family.

There are many laws about cooking on *Shabbat*. Observant people will not turn on the oven or cooktop so their Saturday '*Shabbat* lunch' dishes must be made beforehand. A warm dish like *Cholent* (page 42) cooks over a low heat from Friday afternoon until it is served at lunch the next day. Walking into a home saturated with the aromas of slow cooking immediately connects us with generations of delicious heritage.

All visitors are welcome, in fact it is an especially good deed. There's always another cup of chicken soup in the pot and more room around the table. Hospitality is one of the most important values of our community. The warmth, goodwill and feasting that comes with *Shabbat* carries us through our week.

Challah (page 18), Peri-Peri Chicken Livers (page 27), Egg and Onion (page 24) and Avocado Dip (page 23).

Challah

It's incredibly heartwarming that many of our readers now bake their own *challah* from the recipe in our first book. *Challah* is the golden, egg-enriched plaited bread enjoyed on *Shabbat* and many festivals. It is traditional to serve two loaves on Friday night to represent the double portion of *manna* that sustained Moses and the Israelites in the desert over the day of rest. We love it served with Avocado Dip, Egg and Onion, Chopped Herring and/or Chopped Liver for Friday night starters. — MMCC

500 g (3⅓ cups) plain flour, plus extra
9 g (1½ sachets/3 teaspoons) dried yeast
60 g (¼ cup/2 oz) caster sugar
250 ml (1 cup) warm water
60 ml (¼ cup) oil
1 egg, beaten
3 teaspoons salt

also needed
1 egg, beaten, to glaze
poppy seeds or sesame seeds

Line a large baking tray.

Place the flour in the bowl of a stand mixer (or a large bowl if making by hand). Make a large well in the flour and add the yeast and 2 teaspoons of the sugar. Add the warm water to the well and stir to combine with the yeast and sugar, keeping the liquid in the well. To ensure the yeast is active, leave for 10 minutes or until foamy.

Add the oil and egg to the mixture in the well, stirring with a wooden spoon. Leave for a further 5 minutes. Stir in the remaining sugar and the salt and, using the wooden spoon, gradually incorporate the flour into the mixture in the well. Once combined, using the dough hook attachment of the stand mixer, knead on low–medium speed for 10 minutes until you have a soft, sticky dough that comes away from the sides of the bowl. You can also knead by hand for 10 minutes on your benchtop; you will need to add extra flour but add as little as possible to avoid toughening the dough.

Cover the bowl with plastic wrap and a tea towel. Set aside in a warm place to rise for 2 hours or until it has at least doubled in volume. With a dough scraper or lightly floured hands, tip the dough onto the benchtop and punch down to deflate. Shape into a ball, return to the bowl, cover and leave to rise for a further 1 hour.

When the dough has risen, remove with a dough scraper or floured hands and place on a very lightly floured benchtop. Divide the dough in two to make two loaves.

You will need to shape each piece of dough into a plaited or round loaf. The easiest is a standard 3-strand plait but we currently love the 4-strand plait.

To make a 4-strand plait, divide one piece of dough into four pieces. Take one of the four pieces and, with the palm of your hands moving back and forth over the dough and applying light downward pressure, roll it on the benchtop into a strand (or snake), around 20 cm (8 in) in length. Do not add too much flour to the benchtop, if at all, as you need some friction to roll. Repeat with the remaining three pieces so you have four strands.

To start, place the four strands next to each other lengthways on the benchtop. Pinch the strands together at the top and tuck under slightly.

Take the two outside strands and, starting with the right, cross each to the opposite side.

Take the first from the left (the same strand you just crossed over from the right) and place it in 'the middle'.

Then, take the second from the right across.

And the first from the right to the middle.

Second from the left across.

And first from the left to the middle.

Repeat until the plait is finished.

Pinch the ends of the strands together and tuck under.

Repeat with the second piece of dough to make two plaits. If, for *Rosh Hashanah* and *Yom Kippur*, you want to make two round *challahs*, roll one piece of dough into a long strand and coil it around itself to form a large circle. Tuck the end underneath and press to seal. Repeat with the second piece of dough to make a second loaf.

Place the loaves on the prepared baking tray, cover with a clean, light tea towel and leave to rise for 1 hour. Preheat the oven to 180°C (355°F) conventional.

Brush the *challah* with the beaten egg to glaze and sprinkle with the seeds. Bake for 35 minutes, or until golden. Remove from the oven and allow to cool.

Makes 2 loaves, each serving 8

TIP: Baking your own *challah* is a *mitzvah* (good deed). To recite the special *Hafrashat* blessing, you will need to multiply this recipe by four, using 2 kg (4 lb 6½ oz) plain flour. Before baking the *challah*, remove a small piece of dough, wrap it in foil and burn it.

SEE IMAGE *page 20.*

Top to bottom, left to right: Chopped Herring Salad; Avocado Dip; Egg and Onion; and Chopped Liver.

Avocado Dip

I'm not quite sure how avocado dip ('guac') became such a normal, everyday *shmear* at *Shabbat* tables, but it seems to be routinely found alongside the *challah*. This is our favourite version, especially when avocados are at their best. The recipe came from our good friend, Dr. Jeffrey Engelman, who first made it for me many (many!) years ago. — NATANYA

2 ripe avocados
¼ red onion, finely chopped
1 small roma tomato, seeded and chopped
a good splash of Tabasco sauce or hot chilli sauce
juice of ½ lemon
½ teaspoon salt
¼ teaspoon ground black pepper

Peel and roughly mash the avocado using a potato masher or a fork, trying not to make it too smooth. Add the onion, tomato, Tabasco, lemon juice, salt and pepper. Mix well and season generously to taste with extra salt, pepper, lemon and Tabasco.

Serve with *Challah* (page 18).

Serves 6 as a starter

Chopped Herring Salad

We laughingly say we don't need a DNA test to check if we're Ashkenazi — just wave a bowl of chopped herring in front of us and watch the reaction. Exceptionally popular with the South African Jewish community, along with any other variation of herring, it reflects their mainly Lithuanian heritage. Chopped herring is savoury, salty and sweet. — MMCC

1 slice (70 g/2½ oz) *challah* with crust removed
60 ml (¼ cup) white vinegar
250 g (approx. 3 fillets/8¾ oz) matjes herring fillets
¼ white onion, roughly chopped
1 Granny Smith apple, peeled and quartered
2 eggs, hard-boiled
1 teaspoon sugar
½ teaspoon salt
¼ teaspoon ground black pepper

Put the *challah* in a small bowl and pour over the vinegar. Set aside to soak.

Meanwhile, put the herrings and onion in a food processor and pulse until roughly chopped. Drain and roughly tear the soaked *challah* into pieces. Add the apple, 1 of the eggs, soaked *challah*, sugar, salt and pepper to the herring mixture. Pulse till roughly combined. Do not overprocess, taking care not to puree. Taste for salt, pepper and sugar and add more if needed.

Transfer to a serving dish and grate the remaining egg on top. Serve immediately or refrigerate for up to 4 days.

Serve with *Challah* (page 18) or crackers.

Serves 4–6 as a starter

TIP: If you buy salted herring fillets, you will need to soak them in cold water for 1 hour and rinse before using. If you buy the frozen or refrigerated fillets in oil, no soaking is needed but you may need to defrost them. This recipe is also good made in a mincer.

Egg and Onion

Some of our most treasured recipes have become iconic since we published our first book. To my greatest *nachas* (unbridled joy), this is one of them. It is quite extraordinary that, now, around the world, people serve my grandmother's exceptional (oil-based) Egg and Onion at their *Shabbat* table instead of the more common mayo-based version. It is best made and served on the same day, but if you have any left over, it is still wonderful *shmeared*, with a little butter, on a cracker the next day.
— LISA

1 large onion, chopped
60 ml (¼ cup) oil
¼ teaspoon salt
4 eggs, at room temperature
ground black pepper

Put the onion and oil in a medium frying pan over medium heat and fry for at least 20 minutes or until golden brown, soft and starting to caramelise around the edges. Add the salt and mix.

Meanwhile, place the eggs in a medium saucepan, cover with cold tap water and bring to the boil. As soon as the water starts to boil, set the timer for 8 minutes and reduce the heat to a light boil. At the end of the cooking time, remove the saucepan from the heat, drain and allow cold running water to flow over the eggs for a minute or so. When just cool enough to handle, peel the eggs and, using the coarse side of a box grater, grate into a large bowl.

Spoon the onion onto the grated egg, leaving most of the oil in the pan. Using a wooden spoon or spatula, stir to combine the onion and egg, tasting as you go. Season generously with extra salt and pepper. If it is too dry, add a little oil from the pan. The mixture should easily stick together if pressed with your hand, but should not be overly oily.

Tip the mixture into a serving bowl and cover with plastic wrap until ready to serve, pressing the wrap onto the surface so it doesn't dry out.

Serve at room temperature with *Challah* (page 18).

Serves 4 as a starter

TIP: If serving as a starter with other dishes, use 1 egg per person. This recipe multiplies easily.

SEE IMAGE *page 22.*

Chopped Liver

'What am I, chopped liver?' The often-maligned chopped liver seems to have been relegated to a quick *shmear* and an even quicker quip, but we really think it should have hero status on the *Shabbat* table. Nothing beats a well-seasoned chopped liver made with golden fried onions, sweet *kiddush* wine and old-school *schmaltz*. This recipe came to us from MMCC founding co-author, Paula Horwitz, and the chief cook in her household, husband Gary. — MMCC

250 g (9 oz) chicken livers
1½ tablespoons oil
2 tablespoons *schmaltz* or extra oil
2 onions, sliced
½ teaspoon salt
¼ teaspoon ground black pepper
1 tablespoon sweet sacramental wine or port
3 eggs, hard-boiled

Wash the chicken livers under running water and drain. Lay them out on paper towel for a few minutes to dry.

Heat the oil and *schmaltz* or extra oil in a medium frying pan over high heat. Add the onion and toss. Reduce the heat to medium and sauté the onion for 20 minutes or until soft and lightly golden. Increase the heat to medium-high and add the livers, salt and pepper. Cook for 5 minutes, tossing occasionally, or until the livers are well browned and just cooked through. Add the wine and mix through. Set aside to cool.

Tip the liver and onion mixture into the bowl of a food processor. If you don't have a food processor, you can also use a box grater or mincer. Pulse several times to chop the mixture, taking care not to puree. Grate the eggs using a box grater and add two-thirds of the egg to the processor, setting aside the remaining egg. Pulse again a couple of times to combine. Season to taste with extra salt and pepper and process a little more, as needed, to form a chunky mixture. Spoon into a serving bowl and top with the reserved grated egg.

Store in the fridge for up to 3 days.

Serves 4 as a starter with **Challah** *(page 18)*

TIP: *Schmaltz* is rendered chicken fat — see Kitchen Notes (page 14) for how to make it at home. Chopped liver is also excellent on a bagel (or a Vita-Weat cracker!) with sliced dill pickles.

SEE IMAGE *page 22.*

Peri-Peri Chicken Livers

Over the years I have become so attached to this recipe. I call it the 'chicken liver gateway' dish because every person who has come to my place and told me, 'I don't eat liver', has fallen head over heels in love with this dish. It pairs perfectly with *challah* at the *Shabbat* table, and is on repeat when I have friends over, served with golden, crisp sourdough toasts. — LISA

250 g (9 oz) chicken livers
2 tablespoons oil
2 teaspoons peri-peri or chilli oil
1 onion, chopped
1 clove garlic, crushed
½ teaspoon finely grated fresh ginger
½ teaspoon salt
¼ teaspoon ground black pepper
60 ml (¼ cup) tomato sauce (ketchup)
1½ tablespoons sweet sacramental wine or port
125 ml (½ cup) water

Wash the chicken livers under running water and drain. Lay them out on paper towel for a few minutes to dry.

Heat 1 tablespoon of the oil in a medium frying pan over medium heat. Working in batches so as not to overcrowd the pan, add livers and cook for a few minutes or until browned on all sides and almost cooked through. Take care as they will spit. Remove from the pan and set aside.

Reduce the heat to medium-low and add the remaining oil and the peri-peri or chilli oil to the pan. Add the onion and cook for 20 minutes or until golden and soft. Add the garlic, ginger, salt and pepper and stir for a minute or so until fragrant. Add the tomato sauce, wine or port and water, stirring to combine, and bring to the boil.

Reduce the heat to medium-low and simmer for 20 minutes or until the sauce has thickened and the flavours are well combined. If the sauce dries out before the time is up, reduce the heat, add a little more water and continue to cook.

Return the liver and any juices to the pan and simmer for a further 10 minutes or until thickened and the oil starts to separate. While the livers are cooking, use the flat edge of a wooden spoon or spatula to break each liver up into a few pieces. Season to taste, stir, and cook for a few more minutes.

Serve warm or at room temperature with *Challah* (page 18). Store leftovers in the fridge for up to 2 days.

Serves 4 as a starter

TIP: The sauce can be made well ahead and frozen until ready to use. If you like it very spicy, add 1 bird's-eye chilli, seeded and chopped, with the garlic.

Persian Fish Pilau

A super-fragrant one-pot dish packed with spices, rice, succulent fish and heritage, nodding to the rich food culture of Sydney's Baghdadi-Indian Sephardic community. – MMCC

2 heaped teaspoons garam masala
1 teaspoon ground turmeric
1 teaspoon salt
½ teaspoon ground pepper
600 g (1 lb 3 oz/approx 3) thick white fish fillets (like barramundi), skinned
2 tablespoons oil
2 onions, sliced
1 heaped teaspoon grated fresh ginger
1 clove garlic, crushed
2 large (approx 375 g/13 oz) carrots, peeled and grated
165 g (¾ cup) basmati rice
330 ml (1⅓ cups) water

to serve
small handful coriander leaves
flaky salt

Preheat the oven to 180°C (355°F) conventional. You will need a 2.5 litre (10 cup) flameproof casserole dish with a tight-fitting lid.

Combine the garam masala, turmeric, salt and pepper in a small bowl to make a spice mix. Cut each fish fillet into two or three large pieces. Using around 1 teaspoon of the spice mix, sprinkle it on each side of each piece. Set the remaining spice mix aside.

Heat 2 teaspoons of the oil in the casserole over high heat. Quickly sear the top side of the fish pieces until just golden. You may need to do this in batches to not overcrowd the dish. Remove and set aside.

Reduce the heat to medium. Put the remaining oil in the casserole and sauté the onion for 15 minutes or until light golden. Add the ginger, garlic and remaining spice mix and sauté, stirring, for a minute or so, until fragrant. Add the carrot and cook for 5 minutes, or until well softened, tossing from time to time.

Place the rice in a colander and rinse under plenty of running water. Add the rice to the carrot mixture and toss through for a minute or so until the rice starts to toast a little. Add the water, increase the heat and stir to combine. Once it comes to the boil, remove from the heat and slip in the fish pieces, browned-side up, in one layer, partially burying them in the rice. Cover with a piece of baking paper and the lid (or a double layer of foil if you don't have a lid) and place in the oven for 20 minutes. Remove from the oven, keeping the dish tightly covered, and leave to sit for 10 minutes to finish cooking.

Sprinkle with coriander leaves and flaky salt to taste.

Serves 4

Salmon Crumble

The coarse crumble topping on this salmon is like a little doona (duvet) sealing in moisture to create a golden herby topping with super succulent fish underneath. It also tastes great at room temperature, so you can make it just before *Shabbat*, then deliver it to the table stress-free. – MMCC

800 g (1 lb 12 oz) sustainably sourced salmon (in 4 fillets or 1 piece), skinned and pin-boned
160 g (5½ oz) slightly stale sourdough bread with crust removed
1 clove garlic, peeled
1 long red chilli, seeded and roughly chopped
½ cup loosely packed fresh dill fronds
½ cup loosely packed flat-leaf parsley leaves
½ cup loosely packed basil leaves
60 ml (¼ cup) extra-virgin olive oil
juice of ½ lemon
1 teaspoon salt
¼ teaspoon ground black pepper

Preheat the oven to 180°C (355°F) conventional. Line a baking tray.

Arrange the salmon piece or fillets, touching each other side-by-side, on the prepared tray.

Put the bread in the bowl of a food processor with the metal blade and pulse to form coarse chunks. Add the garlic, chilli, dill, parsley and basil and pulse until the herbs are roughly chopped. Add 2 tablespoons of the oil, the lemon juice, salt and pepper and pulse just until the mixture forms a coarse crumb and is well combined. (Do not pulse for too long, the mixture should still look like bread and herbs, rather than a paste.)

Press the crumb mixture firmly on top of the salmon. Drizzle with the remaining oil and roast for 15 minutes (for rare) or 20 minutes (for medium). Remove from the oven and loosely cover with foil for at least 30 minutes to rest.

Serve just warm or at room temperature.

Serves 4

'Not Fried' Lemon Garlic Chicken

This recipe puts a big tick in the 'I'm too busy to cook on Friday' box. It is a perfect marriage between garlic bread and chicken schnitzel but without the effort and mess of either. Just one bite through the crunchy layer of golden, lemony, garlicky breadcrumbs into the succulent chicken will make you smile. It has quickly become a family favourite in each of our homes. – MMCC

8 chicken thigh fillets
2 tablespoons mustard
160 g (5⅔ oz) sourdough bread with crust removed
finely grated zest of 2 lemons
2 cloves garlic, crushed
1 teaspoon salt
½ teaspoon ground black pepper
1 small bunch chives, roughly chopped
1 small handful flat-leaf parsley, roughly chopped
60 ml (¼ cup) extra-virgin olive oil

to serve
Spicy Cabbage Slaw (page 45)

Preheat the oven to 200°C (390°F) conventional. Line a baking tray.

Coat the chicken thighs with the mustard and place on the prepared tray, smooth-side up, leaving a little space between each.

Place the bread, lemon zest, garlic, salt and pepper in a food processor and process until it forms breadcrumbs. Add the chives, parsley and oil and pulse two or three times until just combined.

Top the chicken pieces with the crumb mixture. Press the crumbs firmly onto the surface of each piece ensuring the chicken is evenly covered with a thick layer. (This can be done a few hours ahead and refrigerated until ready to cook.)

Cook for 35 minutes or until the crumbs are golden on top and the chicken is cooked through.

Serve hot or at room temperature, with Spicy Cabbage Slaw.

Serves 4–6

Chicken Sambal

Our Sephardi friends grew up with curries and sambals, pilafs and biryani. We can't say the same for us Ashkenazi families. The first time we tasted their home cooking, we were blown away by a world of fragrant exotic spices and blends. We thank their community for introducing us to a whole new Jewish food culture, through the beautiful spice shops that popped up in our local areas, and through their recipes. This wonderful sambal is also a story of immigration to a foreign country and of the importance in reviving the recipes of a childhood interrupted and disturbed by war. – MMCC

sambal sauce
400 g (14 oz) tin diced tomatoes
2 mild long red chillies, seeded and chopped
2 onions, finely chopped
2 tablespoons oil
2 cloves garlic, crushed
2 tablespoons kecap manis (sweet soy)
2 kaffir lime leaves
1 stalk lemongrass, quartered and smashed
1 teaspoon tamarind paste

chicken
1 kg (2 lb 3 oz) skinless chicken thigh fillets, each cut into three pieces
½ teaspoon salt
⅛ teaspoon ground black pepper
1 tablespoon oil

to serve
sliced shallots (spring onions)
1 long red chilli, seeded and sliced
chopped coriander leaves
Cucumber Salad (page 229)
steamed basmati rice

To make the sambal sauce, place the tomatoes and chilli in a blender or food processor (or use a stick blender) and blend to form a paste. Set aside.

In a deep, wide frying pan over medium heat, sauté the onion in the oil for about 15 minutes or until light golden and soft. Add the garlic and cook for another minute, then add the tomato mixture and stir in the kecap manis, kaffir lime, lemongrass and tamarind. Continue cooking, stirring from time to time, for 30 minutes or until the mixture has become a rich sauce.

Meanwhile, season the chicken pieces with the salt and pepper. Add the oil to another frying pan over high heat. Working in batches, add the chicken and cook for a couple of minutes until browned on each side. The chicken will still be raw inside. Remove from the heat and set aside.

To finish the dish, heat the sambal sauce over medium heat until it simmers. Add the chicken to the sauce and cook, uncovered, for 20 minutes, until the chicken is cooked through and the sauce has thickened.

Sprinkle with shallots, chilli and coriander leaves. Serve with Cucumber Salad (best with chives for this dish, and don't forget to add them like we did in the photo here!) and steamed basmati rice.

Serves 6

TIP: Make the sauce ahead of time and refrigerate or freeze until needed. The sauce also works well with fish.

Slow-Roasted, French-Style Roast Chicken

Tarragon was never my number-one herb, but one day, on a creative whim, I sprinkled a few leaves of it in the cavity of a chicken. Suddenly the kitchen smelled like the alluring offerings of the Paris *traiteurs* I would walk past on grey, icy winter days in the 1980s, truly the best takeaways of all. I now cook my chicken at a lower temperature so it can be popped in the oven before *Shabbat* to slowly roast until dinnertime. The result is a super-moist, tender roast chook. — MERELYN

1 x 1.6 kg (3½ lb/size 16) whole chicken
2 sprigs fresh tarragon, chopped
8 sprigs thyme, leaves only
2 sprigs rosemary, leaves only
4 sprigs flat-leaf parsley, leaves only
½ lemon
2 tablespoons dijon mustard
1 teaspoon salt
½ teaspoon ground black pepper
8 French shallots (eschallots), peeled
60 ml (¼ cup) extra-virgin olive oil
125 ml (½ cup) white vermouth or white wine

Preheat the oven to 130°C (265°F) conventional.

Take the chicken out of the fridge 1 hour before cooking to bring it to room temperature.

Roughly chop the herbs and mix together. Cut a slice off the lemon half. Add half the herbs and the lemon slice to the cavity, then tie the legs together with kitchen twine.

Place the chicken, breast-side down, in a roasting pan. Using a pastry brush, spread 1 tablespoon of the mustard all over the back of the chicken, sprinkle with some of the salt and a grind of pepper, then sprinkle on some of the remaining herbs. Turn the chicken over so it is breast-side up, spread with the rest of the mustard, then squeeze the lemon juice from the remaining lemon over the top. Season with the remaining salt and a good grind of pepper, then sprinkle the remaining herbs on top. Arrange the shallots around the chicken and drizzle the chicken and shallots with the oil.

Place in the oven and roast for 2 hours 30 minutes–3 hours, basting every hour or so. After 2 hours, add the vermouth or wine to the pan. After 2 hours 30 minutes, check if the chicken is cooked by piercing the thigh just near the drumstick joint. The juices should run clear and a meat thermometer inserted at the thigh joint should read at least 75°C (167°F). If the juices do not run clear, continue to cook. If the pan is looking dry, add a little hot water. If you prefer the skin more crisp, turn the oven to grill for the last 5 minutes of cooking.

When the chicken is cooked, remove from the oven, cover loosely with foil and leave to rest for 15 minutes before serving.

Serves 4

TIP: For a faster cooking time, roast at 180°C (355°F) conventional for 1 hour.

Glazed Roman Lamb Shoulder

We're a slow-roasted-lamb-shoulder sort of a family, especially for Friday night dinner, and this one is my absolute favourite. It has that perfect balance of slightly sweet, slightly spicy and the meat itself is ever so succulent. — MERELYN

2 kg (4½ lb) shoulder of lamb, bone-in
3 cloves garlic, crushed
1 teaspoon salt
1 teaspoon dried oregano
1 teaspoon fresh rosemary leaves, finely chopped
2 tablespoons extra-virgin olive oil

sauce
3 onions, roughly chopped
2 tablespoons oil
1 teaspoon sweet paprika
½ teaspoon cayenne pepper
400 ml (13½ fl oz) tomato passata or puree
250 ml (1 cup) water
2 tablespoons white vinegar
2 tablespoons worcestershire sauce
2 tablespoons brown sugar
1 teaspoon salt

to serve
Smashed Turmeric Potatoes (page 44)

Preheat the oven to 200°C (390°F) conventional. You will need a roasting pan large enough to hold the shoulder.

In a small bowl, mix together the garlic, salt, oregano and rosemary. Place the lamb in the roasting pan. Tip the herb mixture onto the lamb and massage it into the meat. Pour the oil over the top and roast, uncovered, for 1 hour.

Meanwhile, make the sauce. In a large frying pan over medium heat, sauté the onion in the oil for 20 minutes or until golden and soft. Add the paprika and cayenne pepper. Stir for a minute or so and then add the tomato passata or puree, water, vinegar, worcestershire sauce, brown sugar and salt. Cook for 5 minutes, stirring from time to time. Set aside.

After the lamb has been in the oven for 1 hour, reduce the temperature to 120°C (250°F) conventional.

Pour the sauce over the lamb, and cover with a piece of baking paper, then a double layer of foil. Return to the oven and cook for a further 5 hours, basting occasionally, or until fork tender.

Serve with Smashed Turmeric Potatoes.

Serves 4–6

TIP: This dish needs 6 hours in the oven, so plan your time carefully or make it ahead of time and reheat.

Slow-Cooked Roast Beef

We're the first to admit that getting everything on the table, well-cooked and hot, on a Friday night can be challenging, especially when *Shabbat* starts early in the middle of winter. Slow-cooked roast beef guarantees a tender, succulent roast (no drying out here!) and is a super easy main course that can feed a crowd. This dish is fast to prep, making it a really good choice for a busy Friday. — MMCC

130 g (½ cup) seeded mustard
3 tablespoons flaky salt
80 ml (⅓ cup) extra-virgin olive oil
2 kg (4 lb 6 oz) piece scotch fillet beef, tied (see TIP)
2 cloves garlic, peeled and halved

to serve
Everyday Green Salad (page 44)

You will need a medium roasting pan.

In a small bowl, make a paste with the mustard, salt and 1 tablespoon of the oil. Place the beef in the pan. Rub the cut sides of the garlic over the meat and throw the cloves into the pan. Rub the paste over all sides of the beef and drizzle with the remaining olive oil.

Leave the beef to sit at room temperature for 1 hour before cooking.

You can marinate the beef several hours ahead (or overnight) in the fridge, but be sure to take it out 1 hour before cooking.

Preheat the oven to 120°C (250°F) conventional.

Roast the beef for 2 hours or until a meat thermometer shows that the internal temperature is in the range of 58°C (136°F) for rare to 62°C (144°F) for medium.

Leave to rest in the pan for 20 minutes, loosely covered with a piece of foil, before carving. Serve with the Everyday Green Salad.
Serves 8–10

TIP: To ensure the beef retains a good shape and to keep the juices in, tie the piece at regular intervals with cooking twine, or ask your butcher to do it for you.

Ashkenazi *Cholent*

On one hand this is a simple, slow-cooked, super-hearty bean and beef stew, which easily feeds a crowd. On the other hand, it is one of the most utterly Jewish dishes, which tells the story of *shtetl* life in generations past. Seen on many *Shabbat* lunch tables, it allows the cook to observe the laws of *Shabbat* that prohibit 'work'. Placed in the oven before sundown on Friday to cook at a very low temperature overnight, the flavours become deeper as the hours pass by and the aroma fills your home with the essence of Jewish cooking. – MMCC

100 g (½ cup) dried butter (Lima) beans or cannellini beans
100 g (½ cup) dried red kidney or borlotti beans
60 ml (¼ cup) *schmaltz* (see Kitchen Notes, page 13) or oil
3 teaspoons salt
450 g (1 lb) beef top rib or beef short rib
350 g (12½ oz) gravy (stewing) beef, cut into large pieces
¼ marrow bone, sawed in pieces
2 onions, chopped
1 clove garlic, crushed
1 tablespoon ground sweet paprika
½ teaspoon ground black pepper
75 g (⅓ cup) pearl barley
2 carrots, peeled and cut into chunks
2 potatoes (such as desiree), peeled and cut into eighths
500–750 ml (2–3 cups) water

Start this recipe 2 days before. You will need a large (at least 4 litre/16 cup) flameproof casserole dish, preferably with a lid.

Wash the beans thoroughly, place in a bowl and cover generously with tap water. Allow to soak overnight.

Preheat the oven to 110°C (230°F) conventional.

Heat the *schmaltz* or oil in the casserole dish over medium heat. Sprinkle 1 teaspoon of the salt over the meat and bones. In batches, brown the meat and bones in the *schmaltz* or oil on all sides and set aside. Add the onion and fry until golden. Add the garlic, paprika, remaining salt and pepper and toss through the onion. Cook for a minute or until fragrant. Put the meat and bones back in and bury them under the onion.

Drain the beans, rinse and drain again. Add the beans, barley, carrot and potato to the dish. Add enough of the water to reach 1 cm (½ in) below the top of the ingredients. Bring to the boil, place a piece of baking paper on the surface and cover with the lid (or 2 tight layers of foil if there is no lid).

Cook at 110°C (230°F) conventional for 1 hour, then reduce the heat to 100°C (210°F) conventional and cook for 19 hours, checking from time to time. If it looks like it is drying out, add a little water.

Serve hot.

To serve later, leave to cool and refrigerate for up to 4 days, then reheat to serve.

Serves 6

TIP: If you plan to eat the *cholent* for Saturday lunch, put it in the oven by 3pm Friday. If you need to use the oven during the slow *cholent* cooking time, you can take it out for an hour or two and then continue when you are able.

Smashed Turmeric Potatoes

Decades ago we fell in love with turmeric potatoes, then we fell in love with smashed potatoes. Now we have made the perfect *shidduch* (match) and created smashed turmeric potatoes. The orbs of crunchy, well-roasted, super-golden potatoes with fluffy white insides transformed into a golden potato slab is utterly irresistible. — MMCC

1 kg (2 lb 3 oz) baby potatoes
1 teaspoon salt
½ teaspoon ground turmeric
2 tablespoons extra-virgin olive oil
flaky salt, to serve

Preheat the oven to 200°C (390°F) conventional.
Line a roasting pan or baking tray.
Place the potatoes in a large saucepan and cover with water. Add the salt and turmeric and bring to the boil over high heat. Reduce the heat to medium-high and simmer rapidly for 10 minutes or until just starting to soften, then tip into a colander. Leave to drain and dry out in the colander for at least 5 minutes.
Put the potatoes, side-by-side and touching, on the prepared tray and gently squash each potato by pressing down with the bottom of a glass. Drizzle the oil over the potatoes. Roast for 1 hour until crisp and golden.
Sprinkle with flaky salt to serve.
Serves 6

SEE IMAGE *page 39.*

Everyday Green Salad

I make this goes-with-everything salad pretty much every single time anyone eats dinner at home. Perfect for one, easy for a crowd. This recipe makes more dressing than you need for one salad. I like to make a double quantity in a large squeezy bottle which you will always find in my pantry, in reach, ready to shake and drizzle. — LISA

6 baby gem or 1 cos lettuce
1 avocado, peeled and sliced
1 bunch chives, snipped

dressing
160 ml (⅔ cup) extra-virgin olive oil
80 ml (⅓ cup) best-quality red wine vinegar
2 heaped teaspoons dijon mustard
1 teaspoon flaky salt
¼ teaspoon ground black pepper

To prepare the baby gem lettuce, cut the stalk off the bottom and remove any imperfect leaves from the outside. Cut in half through the base and rinse gently. Place in a container lined with paper towel and store in the fridge until ready to eat. If using cos lettuce, cut into quarters through the base, then again across the middle, and wash well. Store the same way.
To make the dressing, combine all dressing ingredients in a jar or squeezy bottle and shake vigorously. Taste for seasoning and add as needed. Store at room temperature (not in the fridge) for up to 1 month.
Just before serving, place the lettuce wedges in a serving bowl or on a platter. Shake the dressing well, drizzle generously over the lettuce and toss gently. Scatter the avocado and chives on top and drizzle with a little more dressing to serve.
Serves 4–6

SEE IMAGE *page 40.*

Spicy Cabbage Slaw

One of my best food memories is going to Katz's Deli in NYC and sitting down to the huge, iconic 'hot pastrami on rye' with coleslaw and Russian dressing and pickled cucumbers on the side. Years later I decided it would be fun to combine all the extra elements into a salad to serve inside the pastrami sandwich. So here it is, a deliciously just-spicy slaw with a sort-of Russian dressing, mustard (normally slathered on the bread) and some sliced pickles to make it complete. – LISA

slaw

250 g (9 oz) cabbage, finely shredded or grated
½ carrot, grated
½ red onion, finely sliced
4 shallots (spring onions), sliced
2 dill pickles, finely sliced

dressing

1½ tablespoons mayonnaise
3 teaspoons dijon mustard
60 ml (¼ cup) extra-virgin olive oil
45 ml (2¼ tablespoons) lemon juice
¾ teaspoon worcestershire sauce
¾ teaspoon sriracha or chilli sauce
½ teaspoon salt
¼ teaspoon ground black pepper

In a large bowl, toss together the cabbage, carrot, red onion, shallots and pickles. To make the dressing, in a separate medium bowl, whisk together the mayonnaise, mustard and olive oil until smooth. Add the lemon juice, worcestershire, sriracha, salt and pepper and whisk to combine. Pour the dressing over the slaw and toss well. Season to taste with salt and pepper.

For a crisp slaw, serve within a few hours of dressing.

Serves 4–6

SEE IMAGE *page 32*.

Olive Oil Chocolate Mousse

This swoon-worthy dairy-free chocolate mousse with a super smooth almost 'nougaty' texture will thrill all chocolate lovers. It also ticks that big box of a do-ahead, crowd-pleasing *pareve* dessert for *Shabbat*. — MMCC

150 g (5⅓ oz) best-quality dark chocolate (70%)
125 ml (½ cup) fruity extra-virgin olive oil or best-quality grapeseed oil
4 eggs, separated
115 g (½ cup) caster sugar
1 tablespoon Grand Marnier (or orange liqueur)
pinch of salt
fresh raspberries, to serve

Start this recipe in the morning or a day ahead. You will need a 1 litre (4 cup) serving bowl or 6 small individual serving bowls.

Melt the chocolate in a double boiler over simmering water (see Kitchen Notes, page 13) then, with a spatula, slowly stir in the oil. Set aside to cool slightly.

Using an electric mixer, beat the egg yolks with half the sugar until pale and fluffy. With a spatula (do not use the machine), slowly stir the chocolate mixture into the egg yolk mixture little by little. Stir in the Grand Marnier. Set aside.

In a separate bowl, using the electric mixer, whisk the egg whites and salt until soft peaks form and gradually add the remaining sugar, whisking until stiff peaks form.

Gently fold half the egg white mixture into the chocolate mixture until just combined. Fold in the remaining egg white mixture. Pour into your large or individual bowls.

Cover and chill for at least 4 hours or overnight. Serve with fresh raspberries.
Serves 6

TIP: If you prefer, simply leave out the Grand Marnier (or orange liqueur). It's important to follow the steps carefully to ensure the chocolate mixture does not seize (split) because if it does, you may, sadly, need to start again. Sometimes it is possible to fix the issue by adding a couple of spoons of boiling water to the mix and whisking well until the mixture becomes smooth again.

Passionfruit Semifreddo

Looking for a *pareve* ice cream that still tastes lush and creamy, but uses neither cream substitutes nor an ice cream machine? This is it. My passionfruit-obsessed family absolutely adore its tropical, sweet yet tart flavour. The texture is best within two days of making. — **MERELYN**

150 g (⅔ cup) caster sugar
finely grated zest of 1 lime
4 eggs, separated
pinch of salt
80 ml (⅓ cup) oil
160 ml (⅔ cup) passionfruit pulp
   (about 7 passionfruit)

This recipe is best started the day before or at least 6 hours in advance. You will need a 1 litre (4 cup) freezer-proof serving dish or container.

In a small bowl, using a spatula, mix the sugar with the lime zest for a minute or so to release the citrus oils. Set aside.

In an electric mixer, whisk the egg whites and salt until soft peaks form, then slowly add half the sugar and continue to whisk on medium speed until stiff. Set aside.

In a separate bowl, whisk the egg yolks and remaining sugar for 5 minutes or until very pale and thick, then gradually add the oil until combined and smooth. Using a spatula, gently fold the egg white mixture into the egg yolk mixture.

Gently fold in the passionfruit pulp. Pour into the serving dish or container, cover and freeze overnight or for at least 6 hours.
Serves 6

TIP: This ice cream contains raw eggs (see Kitchen Notes, page 13).

CHAPTER TWO

Sunday Bagels

In each of our homes growing up, Sunday morning was for bagels. It could have been with smoked salmon and *shmears* or with scrambled eggs and kosher *wurst* (salami, pronounced *voosht*).

As the decades passed, palates expanded and brunch became an easy way to entertain. Along the way we learnt how to make bagels from scratch. There is something quite lovely about the process of kneading, shaping, boiling and baking. And, of course, if it's not a baking day, a quick trip to the shops to buy your favourite bagel is always an option.

When we had young kids, fresh, soft pita stuffed with golden fried falafel, dips and salad from our local Israeli cafe became an easy way to feed a crowd. We've now discovered making pita and falafel at home is actually fun and surprisingly achievable. A truly delicious and worthwhile weekend activity.

Sundays also meant a chocolate yeast *kugelhopf* bought from Sydney's Wellington Cake Shop or Melbourne's Aviv Bakery, reheated at home until the chocolate was molten. Nowadays we like to take it slow in our own kitchens and make a golden, caramelised Cinnamon Brown Sugar Babke (page 72), or a more simple yet rich Chocolate '*Challah* and Butter' Pudding (page 66), to satisfy those chocolatey-doughy-yeasty cravings.

We look back on those early Sunday brunches with heartwarming nostalgia, and hope these recipes inspire you to sit around a table with friends, great food and minimal stress.

Boiled Bagels (page 52) with Salmon Pastrami (page 54), Pickled Red Onion (page 56) and Shmears (page 57).

Boiled Bagels

To boil or not to boil? For us, there's no moving away from the classic Polish technique that creates a chewy and dense, yet soft and light, ring of bready goodness with a glazed and just-sweet crust. Who would have imagined that with a few simple ingredients, you can whip up a batch of bagels at home? It's something we are really excited about and, to all of you thinking 'too hard', we urge you to give it a go. Making these is simply a joy. – MMCC

dough
565 g (3¾ cups/1 lb 3¾ oz) bread flour, plus extra
14 g (2 sachets /1 tablespoon + ½ teaspoon) dried yeast
20 g (1 heaped tablespoon) brown sugar
375 ml (1½ cups) warm water
12 g (2 teaspoons) salt

for boiling
1.5 litres (6 cups) water
60 ml (¼ cup) molasses or brown sugar

for sprinkling
sesame seeds, poppy seeds, 'everything' seasoning and/or flaky salt

It is recommended but not essential to start this recipe the day before so the shaped bagels can be refrigerated overnight.

You will need one or two lined and lightly floured baking trays big enough to fit 12 bagels that will fit in the fridge. The bagels are best eaten on the day of baking.

To make the dough, put the flour in a large bowl (if making by hand) or in the bowl of an electric mixer and make a well in the centre. Add the yeast, brown sugar and half the warm water to the well and stir to combine, keeping the liquid in the well. To ensure the yeast is active, leave to stand for 10 minutes or until frothy.

Add the remaining warm water and the salt to the well and stir to combine. Working the flour in from the sides with a wooden spoon, slowly incorporate it all together.

Once a soft dough forms, turn out onto a lightly floured surface. Knead and stretch the dough with your hands for 10 minutes or until it is smooth and elastic. You can do this with a dough hook in the electric mixer if you prefer. If the dough becomes too sticky, add a little of the extra flour. Put the dough in an oiled bowl. Cover with plastic wrap and a tea towel. Allow to rise in a warm place for 30 minutes.

When the dough has risen, tip it onto a bench and cut into 12 equal portions, about 80 g (2¾ oz) each. Shape each piece into a smooth ball by stretching the dough over itself and tucking it in underneath. Roll each piece into a smooth ball on the benchtop, using light pressure from the palm of your hand. Set the balls aside and allow them to rest for 5 minutes.

Shape the bagels.

Roll one ball into a small sausage, about 18 cm (7 in) long. Wrap the sausage around your fingers, cross the ends slightly and press together to form a ring. Roll the ring, joint-side down, on the bench until you have a reasonably smooth circle. Place the bagel on the prepared tray(s). Repeat with the remaining dough balls and place on the prepared tray(s), making sure there is space between the bagels. Lightly sift a little flour on top and cover with plastic wrap. Refrigerate overnight (or for as long as you have).

When ready to cook the bagels, preheat the oven to 200°C (390°F) conventional.

Pour the water and molasses or brown sugar into a deep frying pan that is wide enough to fit three or four bagels. Bring to the boil over medium-high heat, stirring to dissolve. Remove the bagels from the fridge. Slip them into the water, three or four at a time, smooth-side down. Cook for 1 minute on each side, flipping gently with two forks. Remove carefully from the water and place back on the prepared trays, smooth-side up.

Sprinkle immediately with your choice of seeds and/or salt.

Bake for 20 minutes or until golden brown.

Makes 12 bagels

Salmon Pastrami

This delightful marriage between smoked salmon and the flavours of New York deli pastrami takes Sunday bagels to the next level. Our MMCC co-author (*It's Always About the Food,* 2017), Lynn Niselow, introduced us to her awesome recipe and we are forever grateful. Every time we make it, we can't believe how easy yet spectacular it is. — MMCC

500 g (1 lb 2 oz) sustainably sourced sashimi-grade salmon, skinned and pin-boned

curing mixture
1 tablespoon black peppercorns
1 tablespoon coriander seeds
75 g (¼ cup) salt
110 g (½ cup) sugar

spice crust
3 teaspoons black peppercorns
3 teaspoons yellow mustard seeds
2½ teaspoons coriander seeds

to serve
lemon wedges
extra virgin olive oil
Boiled Bagels (page 52)
Cream Cheese Shallot *Shmear* (page 57)
Pickled Red Onion (page 56)

Start this recipe at least 2 days before serving.

To make the curing mixture, coarsely crush the peppercorns and coriander seeds by carefully pulsing in a mini food processor or spice grinder. In a small bowl, mix the spices with the salt and sugar until well combined.

To make the spice crust, finely grind the peppercorns, mustard seeds and coriander seeds in a mini food processor or spice grinder. Set aside.

To cure the salmon, you will need a large, shallow, non-reactive dish (such as ceramic or glass). Place the salmon in the dish and rub with the curing mixture to cover all sides. Cover with plastic wrap and refrigerate for 24 hours. There will be some liquid in the dish, which you do not need to remove. Turn the salmon over and return to the fridge for another 24 hours.

At the end of the curing time, remove the salmon from the fridge and drain away any liquid. Use the back of a table knife (or a pastry scraper) to scrape off any excess curing mixture.

Press the spice crust onto both sides of the salmon fillet to form a crust. Cover tightly with plastic wrap and refrigerate until ready to slice.

Finely slice the salmon on a 45-degree angle from head to tail. Arrange on a platter with lemon wedges and drizzle with the olive oil.

Serve with Boiled Bagels, Cream Cheese Shallot *Shmear* and Pickled Red Onion.

Keeps for 1 week in the fridge.
Serves around 6, depending on how stuffed you want your bagel

TIP: It's important to use the freshest, sashimi-grade salmon. Ask your fish shop to trim any 'blood lines' for the best result.

Pickled Red Onion

Since we discovered these can't-live-without onions in 2015, we seriously can't live without them! There is always a tub in the fridge ready for every salad, every sandwich and, of course, every bagel stuffed with salmon pastrami and cream cheese shallot *shmear*. – MMCC

3 red onions, thinly sliced
2 green jalapeno chillies, sliced
160 ml (⅔ cup) white vinegar
1 tablespoon lime juice
1 heaped teaspoon salt

Combine the onion and jalapeno in a medium heatproof bowl.

In a small saucepan, combine the vinegar, lime juice and salt. Bring to the boil over high heat, stirring until the salt dissolves, then pour over the onion and jalapeno. Stir well to ensure all the onion comes into contact with the hot liquid. Leave to stand at room temperature for at least 1 hour before using.

This makes a large quantity so store the leftovers in the fridge for up to 1 month

SEE IMAGE *page 58.*

Shmears

We have each spent many a Sunday morning sitting around the table, chatting over the newspapers with a basket of bagels, a platter of smoked salmon and a couple of bowls of our favourite *shmears*. Over the years, the *shmears* have evolved (like us, hopefully!) and these are the ones we go back to, again and again. – MMCC

Cream Cheese Shallot *Shmear*

125 g (4½ oz) cream cheese, at room temperature
1 tablespoon chopped chives
1 shallot (spring onion), finely sliced
1 tablespoon sour cream
1 clove garlic, whole, peeled
⅛ teaspoon salt

Using a wooden spoon, combine all the ingredients in a bowl, mixing well. Refrigerate until needed. Remove the garlic clove before serving.
Makes about ½ cup

SEE IMAGE *page 58.*

Tuna Salad *Shmear*

185 g (6½ oz) tinned tuna in oil, drained
juice of ½ lemon
¼ red onion, finely chopped
4 cornichons (or 1 dill pickle), finely chopped
1 tablespoon mayonnaise
2 teaspoons dijon mustard
⅛ teaspoon salt
⅛ teaspoon ground black pepper

Combine all the ingredients in a bowl, mixing well. Taste for seasoning and adjust as necessary with salt, pepper and lemon.
    This can also be made by pulsing in a mini food processor until combined but still chunky.
Makes about 1 cup

SEE IMAGE *page 59.*

Tel Aviv-Style Falafel
with Pickled Cabbage, Tahina and Pocket Pita

Falafel, the most famous street food in Israel, has become one of our constant cravings, and we think renowned Sydney chef Michael Rantissi's are simply the best … better than all the rest. So imagine how delighted we were when Michael taught Lisa his special recipe (which means, he taught all of us)! We love serving these with Michael's pickled cabbage to cut through the oil, and they are beyond impressive in our homemade pita. And, of course, his tahina sauce which brings it all together. – MMCC

200 g (7 oz/1 cup) dried chickpeas
100 g (3½ oz) dried split broad beans
1 large handful coriander, leaves and fine stems only
2 large handfuls flat-leaf parsley, leaves and fine stems only
1 onion, roughly chopped
1 long red chilli, seeds removed, roughly chopped
4 cloves garlic, roughly chopped
1 teaspoon baking powder
1 teaspoon ground cumin
1 teaspoon ground coriander
3 tablespoons sesame seeds
2 teaspoons salt
oil, for deep-frying

to serve
Pocket Pita Bread (page 63)
Pickled Cabbage (opposite)
Tahina (opposite)

Start this recipe the day before. It is handy, but not essential, to have a traditional falafel spoon.

In a large bowl, soak the chickpeas and broad beans overnight in cold water, changing the water at least twice during this time.

Drain the chickpeas and broad beans and put them in a food processor with the fresh coriander, parsley, onion, chilli and garlic. Pulse several times until it is a grainy but not smooth mixture with the texture of fine couscous. Squeeze a spoonful of the mixture in your hand to check if it holds together. If not, process for longer.

Transfer the mixture to a bowl and add the baking powder, cumin, ground coriander, sesame seeds and salt. Mix together well and taste for seasoning.

Pour enough oil for deep-frying into a medium saucepan and heat until the temperature reaches 170°C (340°F) on a cook's thermometer. Or to test if the oil is hot enough, drop in a cube of bread. It should turn brown in 20 seconds. If the oil is not hot enough, the falafel will break up.

Using a falafel spoon or 2 tablespoons, form the mixture into small patties.

Working in batches, so the oil stays hot and the falafel are well crusted, carefully drop the falafel into the oil and cook for 3 minutes or until deep golden. Using a slotted spoon, remove the falafel and set aside to drain on paper towel. Continue with the remaining mixture.

Serve hot in Pocket Pita Bread, with Pickled Cabbage and Tahina.

Makes about 20 falafel

SEE IMAGE *page 62.*

Pickled Cabbage

¼ head green cabbage
1 tablespoon salt
375 ml (1½ cups) water
250 ml (1 cup) white vinegar

Finely shave the cabbage into a large heatproof bowl. For best results, use a mandolin or the slicing blade in a food processor. Add the salt and massage the cabbage so it starts to wilt and release liquid. Tip off the liquid.
    Combine the water and vinegar in a medium saucepan over high heat and bring to the boil. Pour over the cabbage and toss to ensure the cabbage is well-coated in liquid. Set aside to cool. Serve straight away or leave to ferment in the fridge for up to 3 days for a stronger flavour.
Serves 6

SEE IMAGE *page 62.*

Tahina

100 g (⅓ cup/3½ oz) tahini
juice of ½ lemon
1 clove garlic, crushed
¼ teaspoon salt
ground black pepper
60 ml (¼ cup) water

Combine the tahini, lemon juice, garlic, salt and a little pepper in a bowl and whisk until thick and claggy. Gradually add the water, continuing to whisk until a smooth sauce forms. Season to taste with extra salt, pepper and lemon juice, as needed.
Serves 6

SEE IMAGE *page 62.*

Pocket Pita Bread

260 g (1¾ cups/9¼ oz) bread flour or plain flour, plus extra
1 teaspoon salt
7 g (1 sachet/2¼ teaspoons) dried yeast
¼ teaspoon sugar
180 ml (¾ cup) warm water

Place the flour and salt in a large bowl. Make a well and add the yeast, sugar and water to the well. Stir. Allow to sit for 10 minutes or until it froths. (If you are sure your yeast is still active you can skip this step).

Using a wooden spoon, bring the flour into the well, and mix until a shaggy dough forms. Tip onto a floured bench and knead for about 10 minutes until a slightly sticky, smooth dough forms. If the dough is too sticky, add a little more of the extra flour.

Cut the dough into 12 evenly sized pieces. Gently roll each piece into a ball and allow to rest for 5 minutes.

Spread a clean tea towel on the benchtop. Sprinkle the towel with some extra flour.

On a lightly floured benchtop, using a lightly floured rolling pin, roll each ball into a flat 9 cm (3½ in) circle. Place the dough circles on the floured tea towel and cover with another tea towel to prevent them from drying out. Allow to rise for 1 hour or until the dough circles have almost doubled in thickness.

Preheat the oven to 200°C (390°F) conventional. Place a baking tray in the oven to preheat.

Once the tray is hot, carefully place 6 or so dough circles directly onto the tray, with space in between. Bake for 5 minutes or until puffed. They should be pale and cooked through with a light golden base. Repeat with the remaining dough circles.

Serve fresh. If making ahead, store in an airtight container for up to 3 days and reheat in the microwave or oven to serve.

Makes 12 small pita

Roasted Plum Crumble

In the MMCC kitchen, we have always dreamed of a plum crumble, but we were enjoying our plum cakes so much we wondered if there was actually a need. How wrong we were! There is definitely a great need when gorgeous red plums are in abundance and we want a quick sweet something for everyone to dive into. We've watched our families fight over who is going to scrape the bottom of the dish and devour the sticky, buttery crumble bits swamped in jammy plum juice. – MMCC

8 blood plums, halved, pips removed
150 g (1 cup) plain flour
100 g (3½ oz) unsalted butter, chopped, at room temperature
50 g (scant ¼ cup/1¾ oz) caster sugar
55 g (¼ cup/2 oz, firmly packed) brown sugar
¼ teaspoon salt
whipped cream or vanilla ice cream, to serve

Preheat the oven to 180°C (355°F) conventional. Grease a baking dish large enough to fit the plum halves in one layer.

Place the flour, butter, sugars and salt in a medium bowl and mix together with your fingertips until the butter is evenly dispersed and a rough doughy crumble is formed. The crumble should hold together if squeezed. If not, disperse the butter a little more.

Place the plums, cut-side up, in the prepared dish. Using your hands, sprinkle the crumble on top of the plums, squeezing some of it together to form clumps. Bake for 40 minutes or until the topping is golden brown and the plums are bubbling and well roasted.

Serve warm or at room temperature with cream or ice cream.

Serves 8

Chocolate '*Challah* and Butter' Pudding

There's something deeply satisfying about transforming leftovers into a dish greater than the sum of its parts. Turning Friday's stale *challah* into a warm, chocolatey baked pudding is just the ticket. (Or the leftover slices you've been clever enough to throw into the freezer each week, which now add up to dessert.) This recipe can be prepared the night before so the chocolate custard has time to soak right into the bread. – MMCC

350 g (12⅓ oz) *challah* bread, no crust (approx 1 small round *challah*)
150 g (5⅓ oz) dark chocolate
300 ml (1¼ cups) pure cream
125 ml (½ cup) milk
90 g (½ cup loosely packed) brown sugar
60 g (¼ cup/2 oz) unsalted butter
¼ teaspoon ground cinnamon
⅛ teaspoon salt
2 eggs
cocoa powder, for dusting
vanilla ice cream, to serve

Start this recipe the day (or at least several hours) before.

Grease a 1.5 litre (6 cup) ovenproof dish (you need one that will fit the slices of *challah* snugly).

Slice the *challah* and set aside.

Roughly chop 100 g (3½ oz) of the chocolate. Slice the remaining chocolate into fine shards and set aside. Put the chopped chocolate, cream, milk, sugar, butter, cinnamon and salt in a very large heatproof bowl over a saucepan of simmering water (or you can do this gently in the microwave). Heat gently until the chocolate is melted and all the ingredients are dissolved. Remove from the heat and allow to cool slightly.

In a separate small bowl, whisk the eggs. Add the eggs to the chocolate mixture, a little at a time, and whisk to combine.

Add the sliced *challah* to the mixture and toss to combine, making sure all the slices are fully soaked. You may have to do this in batches.

Put the soaked *challah* into the prepared dish in layers, sprinkling each layer with the fine chocolate shards. Pour any remaining mixture evenly over the top. Make sure the *challah* pieces are covered by the custard as much as possible.

Cover and place in the fridge for up to 24 hours.

When you are ready to serve, preheat the oven to 180°C (355°F) conventional and remove the dish from the fridge.

For a more textured pudding, using a fork, try to bring some of the *challah* corners up so they stick out of the custard. Cover the dish with foil and bake for 25 minutes, then remove the foil and cook, uncovered, for a further 15 minutes until the edges are starting to brown. Remove from the oven and rest for at least 10 minutes before serving.

Dust with cocoa powder and serve warm with ice cream.

Serves 6

Cinnamon Swirl Cake

I talk about my Aunty Myrna a lot; she was the most incredible home cook who sadly left this world too early. I didn't think it was important to get her recipes when I was 18. By the time I was ready, it was too late. I remember sneaking into her kitchen to devour 'Mrs Gunn's *boymeltorte*', a dairy-free cinnamon slab cake with a sugary crust. I have been searching for that recipe for about 30 years, to no avail, but this cake is almost Mrs Gunn's and takes me straight down memory lane. — LISA

cinnamon swirl

60 ml (¼ cup) grapeseed oil or light olive oil
60 g (⅓ cup, lightly packed) brown sugar
1 tablespoon ground cinnamon

cake batter

165 g (1 cup + 1 heaped tablespoon/6 oz) self-raising flour
60 g (½ cup less 1 teaspoon/2 oz) cornflour
⅛ teaspoon salt
3 eggs
255 g (1 cup + 1½ tablespoons/9 oz) caster sugar
135 ml (½ cup + 2 teaspoons/4½ fl oz) oil
1 teaspoon vanilla extract
90 ml (⅓ cup + 2 teaspoons/3 fl oz) orange juice

cinnamon sugar

1½ tablespoons caster sugar
¼ teaspoon ground cinnamon

Preheat the oven to 180°C (355°F) conventional. Line a 20 cm (8 in) square tin with an overhang so you can lift the cake out of the tin.

To make the cinnamon swirl mixture, in a small bowl, combine the oil, brown sugar and cinnamon. Set aside.

Sift together the flour, cornflour and salt. Set aside. Using an electric mixer, whisk the eggs and caster sugar until pale and fluffy. While continuing to whisk, add the oil and vanilla and whisk well. Reduce the speed to low, add the flour mixture and the juice, alternating, in three batches, until well combined.

Pour the cake batter into the prepared tin and drizzle with the cinnamon swirl mixture. Using a fork, swirl it throughout the cake batter, from corner to corner and edge to edge.

Place in the oven and bake for 35 minutes or until golden and a skewer inserted into the centre comes out clean.

While the cake is baking, make the cinnamon sugar by combining the sugar and cinnamon in a small bowl.

When the cake is cooked, remove from the oven and immediately sprinkle the cinnamon sugar on top. Allow to cool then lift out of the tin to serve.

Serves 10

TIP: You can make this in a 20 cm (8 in) round tin instead of the square. Add 10 minutes to the cooking time.

Double Chocolate Chiffon Cake

When I was new to baking, I was looking for a chocolate cake in a hurry. A friend gave me her chocolate chiffon recipe and said 'here, this is the simplest'. I thought, no way, it's too complicated! But, like everything, once you make something once or twice, you wonder what you were nervous about. Once I mastered the technique, it became my go-to, most-often-made cake. After decades of making the original, I have tweaked it to be a little more 'adult' for this book. – LISA

cake
250 g (1⅔ cups/8¾ oz) self-raising flour
40 g (⅓ cup/1½ oz) unsweetened cocoa powder
5 eggs, separated
⅛ teaspoon salt
375 g (1⅔ cups/13¼ oz) caster sugar
210 ml (¾ cup + 1 tablespoon/ 7 fl oz) oil
210 ml (¾ cup + 1 tablespoon/ 7 fl oz) hot water

chocolate buttercream icing
150 g (5¼ oz) dark chocolate, chopped
225 g (8 oz) unsalted butter, at room temperature, chopped
1½ teaspoons vanilla extract
1½ tablespoons glucose syrup
⅛ teaspoon salt
150 g (1 cup + 2 tablespoons) icing sugar mixture

You will need a high-sided angel cake (chiffon) tin that is not non-stick, has a centre funnel and removable base. Do not grease or line it. Before starting the cake, find a bottle that will fit into the top of the funnel – you will need to use this as soon as the cake comes out of the oven.

Preheat the oven to 180°C (355°F) conventional.

Sift together the flour and cocoa and set aside. Using an electric mixer, whisk the egg whites and salt until soft peaks form, then slowly add half the sugar. Continue whisking until just stiff and glossy, then set aside. In a separate bowl, using the same whisk, whisk the egg yolks with the remaining sugar until pale and fluffy. Slowly add the oil and continue to whisk until well combined.

While continuing to whisk on low speed, spoon in the flour mixture, alternating with a little of the hot water, until all the flour and water are incorporated and the mixture is smooth.

With a silicone spatula, gently fold the egg whites into the batter until just incorporated. Pour into the cake tin.

Bake for 1 hour or until the top is just firm to the touch.

After removing the cake from the oven, insert the bottle neck into the funnel and immediately invert the bottle and the tin in one movement so the tin is balancing on the neck of the bottle. The cake will be dangling upside down. Leave until cool to stop it from collapsing.

When completely cool, turn the tin right-side up and run a knife around the outside of the cake and the funnel, literally cutting the cake away from the sides of the tin. Holding the funnel, lift the base out of the tin. Use the knife to cut between the cake and the base. Invert onto a lightweight plate, remove the funnel piece. Invert once again onto your serving plate.

To make the icing, melt the chocolate (see Kitchen Notes, page 13). Set aside to cool slightly.

In the bowl of an electric mixer, beat the butter on medium until pale and creamy. Add the vanilla extract, glucose syrup and salt and beat until combined. On low speed, add the icing sugar, a quarter at a time, scraping down the bowl occasionally, until combined. Add the melted chocolate and mix again until light and fluffy.

Spread the icing over the entire cake.

Serves 12

Cinnamon Brown Sugar Babke

I am completely obsessed with babke. From the aromas of the yeast and then the cinnamon wafting through the kitchen, to the warm, spiced butter as I take a bite, I love everything about the making and eating of babke. The whole process is so comforting. Unlike our previous babkes, this dough uses a simple dough starter, a *tangzhong*, which adds a level of fluffiness and keeps the babke in great shape for several days after baking. This dough is so versatile, you can use it as a base to make a traditional loaf or individual buns with whatever filling you love. — NATANYA

tangzhong starter
100 ml (⅓ cup +1 tablespoon) milk
20 g (1¾ tablespoons) bread flour

dough
260 g (1⅓ cups + 2 teaspoons/ 9¼ oz) bread flour, plus extra
75 g (⅓ cup) caster sugar
7 g (1 sachet/2¼ teaspoons) dried yeast
40 ml (2 tablespoons) milk
1 egg
1 egg yolk
80 g (2¾ oz) butter, melted
½ teaspoon salt

filling
125 g (4¼ oz) softened butter
160 g (¾ cup, lightly packed/ 5⅔ oz) brown sugar
1½ tablespoons ground cinnamon
¼ teaspoon salt

glaze
3 tablespoons white sugar
2 tablespoons water
1 piece orange rind

It is recommended but not essential to start this recipe the day before.

You will need an electric mixer with a dough hook.

To make the *tangzhong*, combine the milk and flour in a small saucepan and whisk to remove any lumps. Cook the mixture over medium heat, stirring constantly, for 2 minutes or until just thickened and resembling wet mashed potato. Remove from the heat and set aside to cool slightly.

To make the dough, combine the flour, sugar and yeast in the bowl of an electric mixer with a dough hook, and make a well. In a separate small bowl, combine the milk, egg, egg yolk and melted butter.

Pour the egg mixture into the well followed by the slightly cooled *tangzhong*. Mix (knead) with the dough hook until all the ingredients have combined. Continue to knead on low speed for about 5 minutes, then set aside to rest for 5 minutes. Add the salt and continue to knead on low for another 10 minutes until you have a somewhat sticky dough. You may need to stop and scrape down the sides once or twice.

With floured hands, remove the dough and give it a few folds before forming a smooth ball. Lightly oil the bowl, put the dough back in, cover with plastic wrap and a clean cloth and leave at room temperature for around 2 hours, depending on the weather, until it is risen and puffy. It will take less time on a hot day. On a cold day, it's best to find a warm place like on top of your clothes dryer or in a cold (off) oven with a dish of hot water placed in the bottom.

Put the covered bowl in the fridge and leave overnight.

The next day, line the base and side of a 20 cm (8 in) round cake tin. If you are using a springform tin, you will also need a lined baking tray to collect any leaks.

To make the filling, combine the butter, brown sugar, cinnamon and salt in a bowl to make a smooth paste. Set aside.

Remove the dough from the fridge and, on a lightly floured benchtop with a lightly floured rolling pin, roll out to form a large horizontal rectangle about 45 x 35 cm (18 x 14 in). Spread the filling evenly over the dough from edge to edge. Starting at the bottom edge, roll the dough evenly into a cylinder.

Using a serrated knife, cut lengthways through the entire roll, so you have two long pieces. Cross the two pieces to make an X with the exposed filling face up, then twist the pieces around each other on either side of the centre of the X to form a twisted log, ensuring the exposed filling is facing up.

Carefully place the twisted log into the prepared tin, roughly joining the ends together to form a circle. Cover loosely with plastic wrap or a clean cloth and leave to rise in a warm place for 1½ hours or until the dough is puffy and lazily bounces back from a poke with your finger. Meanwhile, preheat the oven to 180°C (355°F) conventional.

Place the tin on the prepared tray and bake for 30 minutes. Meanwhile, prepare the glaze.

Combine the sugar, water and orange rind in a small saucepan over medium heat and cook for a few minutes, stirring from time to time, until the sugar has dissolved. Simmer for a few more minutes. Brush the hot syrup over the babke as soon as you have removed it from the oven. Leave to cool in the tin, then remove and serve.

Serves 8–10

SEE IMAGE *page 74.*

Souhariki Biscotti

This recipe, like many in our collection, has had quite a journey. It started with Nanny Rahil in Shanghai (via Harbin, thanks to her Russian parents) who passed it down to her granddaughter, who made it for my next-door neighbour, who made a batch for me. Easy to make, easy to eat and dangerously irresistible. They package up beautifully and make the perfect offering for a friend in need. Plus, they're dairy-free, a bonus for many! Just remember my rule – the ends are always the cook's treat. — LISA

225 g (1½ cups/8 oz) self-raising flour
225 g (1½ cups/8 oz) plain flour
2 eggs
230 g (1 cup/8 oz) caster sugar
185 ml (¾ cup) oil
2 teaspoons vanilla essence
pinch of salt
70 g (½ cup) currants
65 g (½ cup) slivered almonds, toasted

Preheat the oven to 180°C (355°F) conventional. Line a baking tray.

Put the flours in a bowl and whisk to combine. In a separate bowl, whisk together, by hand or with an electric mixer, the eggs and the sugar until well combined and the sugar starts to break down. Add the oil, vanilla and salt and whisk well to combine. Mix in the currants and almonds. Gently mix in the flour until a dough is formed.

Divide the dough into four even-sized pieces, and, with damp hands, roll each piece into a log, around 30 cm (12 in) long. Place the logs side-by-side on the prepared tray, leaving space between them, and flatten slightly with your hands. Bake for 20 minutes, then reduce the heat to 170°C (340°F) conventional and bake for a further 10 minutes, or until just brown.

Remove from the oven, leave the logs to cool for 5 minutes (but no longer). Slice diagonally into 2 cm (¾ in) slices. Place the slices flat on the tray.

Reduce the oven to 110°C (230°F) conventional, and bake for 1 hour for a light golden biscuit or a little longer if you prefer a deep golden brown.
Makes about 50 biscuits

CHAPTER THREE

Rosh Hashanah

JEWISH NEW YEAR

Rosh Hashanah is a celebration of the Jewish New Year, which falls in September or October according to our lunar calendar. We wish each other a *shana tova u'metuka*, a good and sweet new year.

Unlike the Australian fireworks, barbecues and countdown to midnight, our new year is a two-day spiritual festival often marked by attending synagogue and listening to the haunting tones of the *shofar* (a ram's horn that is blown like a trumpet). For many of us, the thought that Jewish people across the world are listening to the same piercing sounds, as we have done for millennia, is deeply connecting.

We celebrate by feasting with family and friends, often with traditional dishes on repeat each year, passed down from generation to generation. Golden honey is the ingredient most often used, to symbolise all the sweetness we want for the year ahead. This is the time to drizzle honey on apples, roast honeyed Carrot *Tzimmes* (page 92), and gift honey cakes. We serve round, often sultana-studded, *Challah* to symbolise the circle of life and continuity.

Ten days later, after a period of repentance, is *Yom Kippur*, the Day of Atonement, the holiest day in the Jewish calendar. Starting the evening before, we fast for 25 hours to repent for any wrongdoings, intentional or otherwise. The time between *Rosh Hashanah* and *Yom Kippur* is a time to acknowledge our mistakes, ask forgiveness and focus on a future filled with good deeds and kindness. We wish each other to be inscribed in the Book of Life.

At the end of *Yom Kippur*, we gather together to break the fast. Some break on a cup of tea and a little something sweet, perhaps our Essential Honey Cake (page 104) or Cinnamon Brown Sugar Babke (page 72). Others launch into a multi-course feast until, holding their bellies, groaning, they roll out the door.

The Essential Honey Cake (page 104) and round *Challah* (page 18).

Fried *Gefilte* Fish

I cannot remember a *Rosh Hashanah* or a *Pesach* without the very Jewish homemade *gefilte* fish, first made by my grandmother and then my mother. Always served with *chrain* (horseradish), it is an essential and expected first course at the *Rosh Hashanah* feast or the *seder*. Sephardi people (and maybe most others) might exclaim that only staunch Ashkenazi Jews (i.e. us) can eat the old-school, boiled, slightly sweet, pale ovals of *gefilte* fish. We tend to agree. This fried version, a little like a salmon patty, will satisfy everyone. — NATANYA

2 tablespoons extra-virgin olive oil
2 onions (1 chopped and 1 grated)
500 g (1 lb 2 oz) mix of perch, bream or cod (or other white fish) fillets, minced
2 eggs
40 g (1½ oz) *challah* breadcrumbs or *matzo* meal
1 tablespoon sugar
2 teaspoons salt
¼ teaspoon white pepper
60 ml (¼ cup) water
30 g (½ cup) panko breadcrumbs or *matzo* meal
oil, for frying

Heat the olive oil in a frying pan over medium heat and sauté the chopped onion for 15 minutes or until soft and light golden. Set aside to cool.

In a bowl, mix together the grated and fried onion, minced fish, eggs, fresh breadcrumbs (or *matzo* meal), sugar, salt and pepper. Add the water and mix to combine. Cover with plastic wrap and refrigerate for at least 1 hour (and up to 24 hours). This is essential.

To cook the *gefilte* fish, you will need a small bowl of water nearby to wet your hands. Place the panko breadcrumbs or *matzo* meal on a plate. With slightly wet hands, make 50 g (2 oz) balls of the mixture and flatten slightly to make a patty. Coat both sides in breadcrumbs or *matzo* meal and set aside.

Add enough oil to a frying pan to reach a depth of about 1 cm (½ in). Heat on medium-high until hot (a small pinch of the mixture put in the oil should sizzle straight away). Working in batches, shallow fry the patties for 3–4 minutes each side until deep golden brown and cooked through. It is a good idea to cut open the first patty to check it is cooked (cook's treat!).
Makes 16 patties

TIP: Ask your fishmonger to mince the fish. The mixture needs to rest for at least 1 hour (and up to 24 hours) before frying.

Chargrilled Maple Soy Salmon

Another iconic recipe from the MMCC collection, this marinade will be one of your 'go-to' recipes forever, as it is ours. The salmon takes on an almost-cured texture after marinating overnight and, when cooked, develops a flavour and sweetness that is a perfect union with the almost-charred crust.
— MMCC

80 ml (⅓ cup) soy sauce or tamari
80 ml (⅓ cup) maple syrup
1 tablespoon freshly grated ginger
1 tablespoon fresh lemon or lime juice
4 x 200 g (7 oz) sustainably sourced salmon fillets, skinned and pin-boned
2 teaspoons extra-virgin olive oil

to serve
Potato Gratin (page 203)

You will need a wide dish or container that fits the salmon fillets in one layer.

Combine the soy or tamari, maple syrup, ginger and lime juice in the dish. Add the salmon, turning a few times to coat in the marinade, and arrange in one layer. Cover and refrigerate overnight (or for at least 4 hours), turning the fillets a couple of times.

Take the salmon out of the fridge 1 hour before cooking. Drain and discard the marinade. Gently dry the fillets with paper towel.

Heat a barbecue flat plate or a non-stick frying pan to medium-high and grease with the oil. Cook the fish, presentation-side down, for 2–3 minutes or until a deep golden crust forms. Using a flat spatula, gently lift up a corner to check the crust. It will only be ready to turn when a crust has formed. Reduce the heat to medium, carefully flip each fillet and cook for 4–5 minutes or until almost cooked through. Set aside to rest for at least 15 minutes.

Serve warm or at room temperature with Potato Gratin.
Serves 4

Spice-Crusted Whole Chicken

Imagine how chuffed we were when Australian cooking doyenne Charmaine Solomon made her late husband's incredible roast chicken for us. In her kitchen! It is an immense joy to dive into this well-spiced and fragrantly crusted, succulent and totally unique roast chicken. The perfect foil to all the sweetness of *Rosh Hashanah*, it is also a delicious insight into our community's Sephardi families who hail from India and Burma. – MMCC

1 x 1.5 kg (3 lb 5 oz) whole chicken, butterflied
2 small sweet potatoes, thickly sliced
1 tablespoon extra-virgin olive oil

spice paste
2 cloves garlic, crushed
2 teaspoons grated fresh ginger
1½ tablespoons curry powder
1 teaspoon sweet paprika
2 teaspoons salt
½ teaspoon ground black pepper
1 teaspoon garam masala
2 tablespoons lemon juice
10 fresh curry leaves
2 teaspoons light soy sauce
2 tablespoons oil
2 tablespoons ground rice or rice flour
3 shallots (spring onions), chopped
1 small handful coriander, leaves and fine stems only, plus ¼ cup extra coriander leaves, to serve

to serve
Yellow Rice (page 99)

To make the spice paste, combine the garlic, ginger, curry powder, paprika, salt, pepper, garam masala, lemon juice, curry leaves, light soy sauce, oil, ground rice or rice flour, shallot and coriander in a food processor and process to make a paste. Add a little warm water, if necessary, to reach a spreading consistency. You can make the paste ahead and store in the fridge.

Rub the chicken all over with the paste, carefully sliding some under the skin on the breast and legs. Set aside to marinate for at least 1 hour at room temperature or in the fridge if longer.

Preheat the oven to 180°C (355°F) conventional. Line a large roasting pan.

Lay the sweet potato slices in the prepared pan and place the chicken on top. Drizzle with the olive oil. Roast, uncovered, for 1 hour or until golden brown and the juices run clear when pierced with a knife at the thigh joint. If the chicken browns too much during cooking, cover with foil.

Remove from the oven and rest for 15 minutes, loosely covered with foil. Sprinkle with coriander leaves and serve with Yellow Rice.
Serves 4

Lamb and Date Tagine

Despite my Ashkenazi heritage, I am drawn to Sephardi flavours like a bee to honey. They just make my taste buds sing, and I search out North African Jewish recipes whenever possible. I was so happy when we were given this warming stew, heady with classic, fragrant Moroccan spices then sweetened with dates. What better way to celebrate a sweet new year? — MERELYN

2 onions, chopped
80 ml (⅓ cup) extra-virgin olive oil
1 teaspoon ground ginger
1 teaspoon ground cinnamon
1 tablespoon ground cumin
½ teaspoon ground black pepper
1.5 kg (3 lb 5 oz) boneless lamb shoulder, trimmed and cubed
180 ml (¾ cup) water or chicken stock
pinch of saffron threads
1 teaspoon salt
½ preserved lemon
2 tablespoons honey
2 tablespoons lemon juice
150 g (5⅓ oz) medjool dates, pitted and halved

to serve
⅓ cup flaked almonds
1 teaspoon extra-virgin olive oil
pinch of salt
coriander leaves
Israeli Rice Pilaf (page 98) or steamed basmati rice

In a heavy-based pan over medium heat, sauté the onion in the oil for around 10 minutes until softened. Add the ginger, cinnamon, cumin and black pepper, and stir until fragrant, about 1 minute. Increase the heat to high, add the lamb and brown on all sides, tossing from time to time.

Add the water or stock, saffron and salt. Reduce the heat to low, cover and simmer for 2 hours, stirring occasionally to prevent the sauce sticking.

Meanwhile, rinse the preserved lemon under cold water, remove and discard the membranes and pulp, and cut into strips.

After the lamb has cooked for 2 hours, stir the honey, lemon juice, dates and preserved lemon into the pan and season to taste with salt and pepper. Cook for another 30 minutes or until the meat is fork tender. If there is too much liquid, leave the lid off for this part of the cooking.

In a small frying pan over medium heat, fry the flaked almonds with the oil and salt for about 2 minutes or until golden. Immediately tip onto a plate to prevent burning.

Sprinkle the lamb with the flaked almonds and coriander leaves.

Serve with Israeli Rice Pilaf or steamed basmati rice.

Serves 6

TIP: It's preferable, though not essential, to make the tagine ahead of time to let the flavours develop and make the lamb more tender.

Pickled Brisket
with Honey Caramelised Onions

This outstanding and unique recipe has been in my life forever. From my memories of eating it in Melbourne at *Rosh Hashanah* way back when, to our first book and beyond, it has been cooked, shared and hallowed by many. It is now truly an iconic MMCC recipe. — LISA

1.5 kg (3 lb 5 oz) pickled or corned beef brisket, rinsed
1 litre (4 cups) water
250 ml (1 cup) white vinegar
185 g (1 cup, lightly packed) brown sugar
1 tablespoon crushed black peppercorns
4 bay leaves
60 ml (¼ cup) extra-virgin olive oil
3 onions, sliced
½ teaspoon salt
¼ teaspoon ground black pepper
90 g (¼ cup) honey
125 ml (½ cup water), for basting

to serve
Braised Red Cabbage (page 94)

You will need a stockpot and a roasting pan big enough to fit the brisket.

Combine 1 litre water, vinegar, sugar, peppercorns and bay leaves in the stockpot. Stir to combine and place the brisket in the liquid. Add enough extra water to cover by 3 cm (1 in).

Over high heat, bring to the boil, then reduce the heat and simmer rapidly, with the lid on, for at least 2 hours or until soft and fork tender. Remove from the heat and allow to cool slightly in the liquid. (If not using immediately, cool completely and refrigerate in the liquid for up to 3 days.)

When ready to roast, preheat the oven to 180°C (355°F) conventional. Drain the brisket, discard the liquid and spices, and place in the roasting pan.

Heat the oil in a frying pan over medium heat and sauté the onion, salt and pepper for 15 minutes, or until soft and starting to brown.

Cover the brisket with the fried onion and drizzle with the honey. Add 125 ml (½ cup) water to the base of the pan, place in the oven and roast for 30 minutes, basting from time to time, until golden.

Slice thickly across the grain (see TIP on page 90). Serve warm or at room temperature with Braised Red Cabbage.
Serves 6–8

TIP: It's essential to buy a pickled or corned brisket, not fresh. Leftovers make spectacular Reuben-style sandwiches on dark rye with Spicy Cabbage Slaw (page 45).

Rosh Hashanah Brisket

This is the perfect dish to celebrate *Rosh Hashanah*. Sweet for the new year with carrots, honey and prunes, and doubly sweet for the cook, because the meat, veggies and carbs are all in one pot. – MMCC

80 ml (⅓ cup) oil
1.5 kg (3 lb 5 oz) well-marbled beef brisket
1 teaspoon salt
¼ teaspoon pepper
4 onions, chopped
3 carrots, peeled and thickly sliced
3 desiree potatoes, quartered
75 g (⅓ cup) pitted prunes
1 cinnamon stick
2 pieces orange rind
90 g (¼ cup) honey
375 ml (1½ cups) chicken stock

to serve
Potato Kugel (page 95)

Start this recipe the day before.

Preheat the oven to 130°C (266°F) conventional.

Heat 1 tablespoon of the oil in a large flameproof casserole dish or roasting pan over high heat. Season the brisket with the salt and pepper, then sear for a few minutes on each side and set aside. Reduce heat to medium, add the remaining oil and fry the onion for 10 minutes or until just starting to brown.

Remove half the onion and set aside, leaving the remainder in the bottom of the pan. Place the brisket on top and top with the reserved onion. Add the carrot, potato, prunes, cinnamon stick and orange rind. Drizzle the honey on top and add enough stock to reach about halfway up the side of the meat. Cover with baking paper and a tight lid (or 2 layers of foil, tightly sealed). Place in the oven and cook for 3 hours.

Remove the lid and the paper and baste with the juices. Check for fork tenderness. If not tender, cover again, and cook for a further 30 minutes or until the meat is fork tender. Leave to cool in the pan.

Once cool, remove the brisket and slice across the grain. Place back in the sauce and refrigerate overnight.

The next day, remove the fat from the top and discard.

Preheat the oven to 180°C (355°F) conventional and cook for 1 hour, uncovered, basting, until the brisket is well glazed and hot. Serve with Potato Kugel.

Serves 6, generously.

TIP: Let's talk brisket for a moment. A whole brisket is made up of two parts: the point (or deckle), which is well marbled, and the flat (or first cut), which is leaner. The challenge of cooking brisket is the flat can easily dry out, as opposed to the point, which transforms into soft, fork-tender meat. Depending on where you buy your meat, you might be able to request your preference. If not, don't stress, cook the whole brisket and let everyone choose their slice.

Our brisket cooking time suggestion is 1 hour at 130°C (266°F) conventional for every 450 g (1 lb) brisket (or until fork tender), plus an extra 1 hour at 180°C (355°F) conventional to serve. It is always better cooked a day or two before with the extra hour just before serving.

It is best to slice the brisket 'across the grain' for maximum tenderness. Identify the direction of the muscle fibres then cut the meat perpendicular to those fibres, creating tender, non-stringy slices. Be aware the direction changes in different parts of the brisket.

Carrot *Tzimmes*

I have been cooking this dish for decades and eating it for even longer. My family recipe for slow-cooked, almost chewy carrots, candied with honey, butter and cinnamon, simply celebrates the traditions of *Rosh Hashanah*. Round carrot slices symbolise coins for a year of prosperity, a generous amount of honey hopes for a sweet year, and all-round deliciousness simply serves up joy. This dish reheats well. — LISA

1 kg (2 lb 3 oz) carrots, peeled
75 g (⅓ cup) sugar
220 g (⅔ cup) honey
juice of 1½ lemons
¼ teaspoon ground cinnamon
½ teaspoon salt
¼ teaspoon ground black pepper
2 tablespoons butter or margarine

Start this recipe the day before serving.

Grease a 1.5 litre (6 cup) baking dish (preferably one you are happy to serve the carrots in).

Cut the carrots into 1 cm (½ in) rounds. Place in a saucepan and add just enough water to come almost to the top of the carrots. Add the sugar, honey, lemon juice, cinnamon, salt, pepper and butter or margarine. Place the pan over high heat and bring to the boil, stirring from time to time. Reduce the heat to medium and cook, uncovered, stirring regularly, for 1 hour or until the carrot is glazed, soft and the water is almost all gone. Season to taste with extra salt, pepper and lemon juice, as needed.

Pour into the prepared baking dish and refrigerate until cold or overnight. (At this point you can refrigerate for several days.)

When ready to serve, take the baking dish out of the fridge about an hour before placing it in the oven. In the meantime, preheat the oven to 200°C (390°F) conventional. Cover the dish with foil and bake for 30 minutes. Remove the foil and bake for a further 15 minutes or until the carrots are golden.

Serves 6 as a side dish

Braised Red Cabbage

A vegetable side dish that is even better when reheated, red cabbage goes extremely well with any roasted meat. It is the perfect choice for the hyper-busy, hyper-organised pre-*Rosh Hashanah* rush we all go through every single year. — MMCC

1 onion, finely sliced
1 tablespoon extra-virgin olive oil
½ small (500 g/1 lb 2 oz) red cabbage, finely sliced
2 Granny Smith apples, grated
2 tablespoons lightly packed brown sugar
2 tablespoons balsamic vinegar
1 tablespoon currants
1 teaspoon salt

In a deep frying pan over medium heat, sauté the onion in the oil for 15 minutes or until soft. Add the cabbage and apple, then toss, cover and continue to cook for 15 minutes or until well softened.

Add the sugar, vinegar, currants and salt and toss to combine. Cook for 20 minutes, covered, stirring from time to time, until the cabbage is soft and everything comes together. Season to taste with extra sugar, vinegar and salt, as needed.

Serves 6–8

SEE IMAGE *page 89.*

Potato Kugel

One thing I have learnt, over the years of preparing the feast for *Erev Rosh Hashanah,* is the more you can get done beforehand, the better. We always, for as far back as I can remember, have potato kugel on our table to serve with the brisket. I make two kugels the day before, one to reheat and serve at night, the other for lunch after *shul* (synagogue) the next day. Thank you Claudia Roden for what is now a firmly instilled family tradition. — NATANYA

4 eggs
1 onion
80 ml (⅓ cup) olive oil or chicken *schmaltz* (see Kitchen Notes, page 13)
1.5 kg (3 lb 5 oz) potatoes, peeled
3 teaspoons salt
¼ teaspoon ground black pepper

Preheat the oven to 180°C (355°F) conventional. You will need a greased 2 litre (8 cup) baking dish, approximately 26 x 18 cm (10 x 7 in).

Crack the eggs into a large bowl and beat. Grate the onion and add to the eggs. Add the oil or *schmaltz* and mix. Grate the potatoes and immediately add to the mixture along with the salt and pepper. Stir to combine. Spoon the potato and its liquid into the prepared baking dish. Sprinkle with extra ground black pepper and bake for 1 hour 10 minutes or until golden brown.

Serves 8

SEE IMAGE *page 96.*

Israeli Rice Pilaf

This side dish of steamed fragrant basmati, studded with fried onion, golden toasted pine nuts and sweet currants, is a fabulous mix of textures and flavours. It is particularly good alongside any saucy, slow-cooked curry or casserole, and the currants add lovely pops of sweetness for *Rosh Hashanah*.
— MMCC

220 g (1 cup) basmati or long-grain rice
2 tablespoons pine nuts
40 g (1½ oz) vermicelli egg noodles
1½ tablespoons extra-virgin olive oil
1 onion, chopped
2 tablespoons currants
310 ml (1¼ cups) chicken stock
½ teaspoon salt

Place the rice in a sieve and rinse under cold running water until the water runs clear.

In a small frying pan over medium heat, toast the pine nuts until golden brown. Set aside. Break up the noodles into short pieces, about 5 cm (2 in) long. In the same pan, heat half the oil and sauté the noodles until golden brown. Take care, they burn easily. Remove from the pan and set aside.

You will need a saucepan with a tight-fitting lid. Place the saucepan over medium heat and sauté the onion, uncovered, in the remaining olive oil for 20 minutes or until golden brown. Add the currants, tossing to combine. Add the rinsed rice and toss for a minute or two until well combined and the rice becomes opaque.

Add the stock and salt, bring to the boil, then cover and reduce the heat to low. Simmer, without stirring, for 15 minutes. Remove from the heat, place a folded tea towel between the saucepan and lid and leave to steam for 5 minutes.

Turn the cooked rice out onto a serving platter and fluff with fork. Top with the fried noodles and pine nuts to serve.

Serves 4–6 as a side dish

SEE IMAGE *page 86.*

Yellow Rice

Decades ago, in an after-school 'cookery class', I learnt how to make Yellow Rice, an eye-opening insight into Sephardi flavours and the first time I ever tasted turmeric. This is more than a Year 9 recipe and I was thrilled when it turned up for our second book. It is the perfect side dish, also honouring the Sephardi kitchen. – **MERELYN**

1 tablespoon olive oil
1 onion, finely chopped
¼ teaspoon ground black pepper
½ teaspoon ground turmeric
220 g (1 cup) basmati rice, well rinsed
375 ml (1½ cups) chicken stock
flaky salt

Choose a medium saucepan with a firm-fitting lid. Heat the oil over medium heat and fry the onion for 15 minutes or until soft and translucent. Add the pepper and turmeric and cook until fragrant, stirring. Add the rice and stir until well coated.

Add the stock to the pan and bring to the boil. Add salt to taste. Cover, reduce the heat to low and cook for 15 minutes, or until the rice is tender. Avoid taking the lid off the saucepan so the rice steams and does not dry out. Fluff the rice to serve.

Serves 4

SEE IMAGE *page 85.*

Baked Apples

There are traditional Jewish foods and then there are beloved recipes that become family traditions. Old-fashioned baked apples became my once-a-year *Rosh Hashanah* dessert in the nineties, with honey cake alongside, of course. They are a warming finish to the *'Rosh'* feast and I love how my family have come to expect them every year. Being a gluten-free dessert is a bonus to my crew – the whole family can eat it. — MERELYN

6 Granny Smith apples
1 tablespoon unsalted butter, at room temperature
2 tablespoons brown sugar
¾ teaspoon ground cinnamon
120 g (¾ cup) sultanas
170 g (¾ cup) caster sugar
100 ml (⅓ cup + 1 tablespoon) water
1½ tablespoons golden syrup
finely grated zest and juice of 1 lemon
vanilla ice cream, to serve

Preheat the oven to 180°C (355°F) conventional. You will need a baking dish that fits the apples snugly in one layer.

Remove the core from the apples with an apple corer. Score (cut into the skin but not into the apple itself) around the middle of the apples with a small knife and set aside.

To make the stuffing, combine the butter, brown sugar and cinnamon in a bowl, then add sultanas and mix to combine. Stuff the cored centre of each apple tightly with the mixture, mounding some on top, and place in the baking dish. Any leftover stuffing can be scattered around the apples.

Combine the caster sugar, water, golden syrup, lemon zest and juice in a small saucepan and stir over medium heat until the sugar dissolves. Taste and add more lemon juice if desired. Pour over the apples, taking care to not break up the mounds of stuffing.

Bake, uncovered, for 45 minutes or until the apples are soft but still holding their shape. You can test with a skewer or a sharp knife.

Serve warm with vanilla ice cream, with some of the syrup drizzled over the top.

Serves 6

TIP: If your sultanas are particularly dry, soak them in boiling water for 30 minutes before draining and using.

Roasted Apple Cake

We've always said, there's something about Jews and cake, but, even more, it's Jews and apple cake. Despite having one in each of our four books, we needed a new recipe that ticked every single one of our many boxes. So we created our own. For us, this is the one. — MMCC

apples
3 large Granny Smith apples, peeled
1 tablespoon unsalted butter
1 tablespoon apple cider vinegar
45 g (¼ cup loosely packed) brown sugar

cake
125 g (½ cup + 2 teaspoons/ 4½ oz) caster sugar
finely grated zest of 1 lemon
120 g (4¼ oz) unsalted butter, at room temperature
2 eggs
½ teaspoon vanilla
150 g (1 cup/5⅓ oz) plain flour
2 teaspoons baking powder
¼ teaspoon salt
100 ml (⅓ cup + 1 tablespoon/ 3⅓ fl oz) pure cream
1 tablespoon coarse cinnamon sugar (see Kitchen Notes, page 13)
whipped cream, to serve

Preheat the oven to 180°C (355°F) conventional. Line a 20 cm (8 in) springform cake tin.

Roughly chop the apples into 1 cm (½ in) dice. Place in a small ovenproof dish with the butter, apple cider vinegar and brown sugar and mix together. Roast for 40 minutes, basting from time to time, until just cooked through. Set aside to cool to room temperature.

Reduce the oven temperature to 170°C (340°F) conventional.

Put the sugar and lemon zest in the bowl of an electric mixer and beat together for a minute or so to release the citrus oils. Add the butter and beat until very pale and creamy. Add the eggs, one at a time, beating well after each addition, then add the vanilla, stopping the mixer and scraping down the sides of the bowl from time to time.

In a separate bowl, sift together the flour, baking powder and salt. Using a spatula, fold it into the butter mixture, followed by the cream.

Using the spatula, gently fold half of the roasted apples and any juices through the cake batter. Spoon into the prepared tin and scatter the remaining apples evenly on top. Sprinkle with the cinnamon sugar and bake for 50 minutes or until a skewer inserted into the centre comes out clean.

Allow to cool and serve with whipped cream.

Serves 8

The Essential Honey Cake

Honey cake is the most traditional and ubiquitous recipe made and enjoyed at *Rosh Hashanah*. Until we published this recipe in our first book, cooks would lament about their dry honey cake, but this one is life changing. We've made it in lots of different shapes and sizes: in Italian-style paper loaf pans as gifts, in muffin tins for the kids, in large silicone tins for a crowd. We've now scaled it down to a small round, perfect for the family, gifting or freezing. – MMCC

dry mixture
115 g (¾ cup) plain flour
115 g (¾ cup) self-raising flour
¾ teaspoon bicarb soda
20 g (2 tablespoons) unsweetened cocoa powder

wet mixture
250 g (scant ¾ cup) honey
170 g (¾ cup/6 oz) caster sugar
90 ml (⅓ cup + 2 teaspoons) oil
2 eggs
½ teaspoon vanilla extract

also needed
185 ml (¾ cup) hot water

This cake is best made 2–3 days ahead of serving.

Preheat the oven to 180°C (355°F) conventional. Line the side and base of a 20 cm (8 in) springform tin.

For the dry mixture, sift the flours, bicarb and cocoa into a bowl. Set aside.

For the wet mixture, using an electric mixer, whisk the honey, sugar, oil, eggs and vanilla together for a few minutes until smooth and well combined. While continuing to whisk on low speed, add the dry mixture into the wet mixture in several batches, alternating with the hot water, until you have a smooth, wet batter.

Place the prepared tin on a baking tray (to catch any leaks) and pour the batter into the tin. Place into the oven and immediately reduce the temperature to 170°C (340°F) conventional. Bake for 1 hour or until just firm to the touch. Allow to cool completely in the tin, then remove and double wrap the cake in foil (so it is airtight) until ready to serve.

Serves 8

TIP: This is a cake to make ahead – it is at its best, and most sticky peak, 2 or 3 days after baking.

Honey Peanut Tuiles

We have made the original version of these delicate yet crisp, chocolate-studded, flat wafer-like biscuits at more cooking demonstrations over the years than any other recipe. Want to know why? It is a simple biscuit to make, it uses ingredients that are found in most pantries, and the prep and cooking time are both short. Plus, everyone adores them! – MMCC

50 g (1¾ oz) unsalted butter, at room temperature
85 g (⅓ cup + 2 teaspoons/3 oz) caster sugar
45 g (1½ tablespoons) honey
40 g (¼ cup + 1 teaspoon/1½ oz) plain flour
1 egg white
50 g (1¾ oz) dark chocolate, roughly chopped
70 g (½ cup) roasted salted peanuts, roughly chopped

Preheat the oven to 180°C (355°F) conventional. Line two medium 38 x 26 cm (15 x 10 in) baking trays.

Put the butter, sugar, honey, flour and egg white in a food processor or blender and process until well combined and completely smooth.

Using a spatula or palette knife, spread the mixture thinly (but not paper-thinly) and evenly onto the prepared baking trays. This is the right amount of mixture for two trays. Sprinkle the chocolate and peanuts evenly over the mixture.

Bake for 15 minutes (we suggest you start checking after 11 minutes, especially the first time you make them) until lightly and evenly browned and cooked through. They will still be soft at this point. Cool completely on the trays until crisp, then break into pieces and store in an airtight container. In humid weather, it helps to store with a silica gel sachet.

Serves 10

TIP: In humid weather, the wafers can soften. If this happens, you can refresh in a hot oven for a few minutes and allow to cool before serving.

CHAPTER FOUR

Sukkot + Harvest

Welcome to one of the most joyous festivals in the Jewish calendar. *Sukkot* celebrates the bounty of the autumn harvest (although it is actually celebrated in spring in Australia) and reminds us of the Israelites' nomadic 40 years in the desert after leaving Egypt.

It is a tradition at this time to build a *sukkah*, a temporary hut with a roof typically made of branches, so the stars can be seen at night while also providing shade from the sun during the day. People love to brightly decorate their *sukkah*. We all grew up excitedly making paper chains from coloured paper strips and Clag (old-fashioned glue for Aussie school kids) to drape from corner to corner.

The aim over this seven-day festival is to spend as much time as possible eating and drinking in the *sukkah* with friends and family. To celebrate the harvest, we cook fresh, colourful and abundant salads and vegetable dishes; a Broccoli Slaw (page 133) studded with sweet currants or Spiced Barbecue Chicken with Green Hummus and Herb Salad (page 120). Dishes that are hearty enough to serve outdoors and plentiful enough to allow delicious leftovers. And there is always the opportunity to pop in for a simple cup of tea and a piece of cake. We also celebrate by eating stuffed dishes such as savoury *Kreplach* in chicken soup (aka Jewish ravioli, page 110) and sweet *Rugelach* pastries (page 140). The concept of 'stuffed' symbolises the bounty of the harvest.

Many people perform the *mitzvah* (good deed) of making a blessing while shaking the *lulav* (a long palm frond with willow and myrtle) and the *etrog* (a large lemon-like citrus, the fruit of a citron tree). Some do this in hope for a bountiful harvest, universal peace or a united community, others do it simply for the ritual.

A beautiful lesson from this festival is that, like a *sukkah*, nothing is permanent, so we need to make the most of every day. And, like the Israelites in the desert, it symbolises our ability to adapt and persevere, to find joy and gratitude, even when life feels uncertain.

Spiced Barbecue Chicken (page 120).

Kreplach

Each time I eat these *kreplach*, they transport me back to my childhood and even further back to those whose legacy I carry with me in the kitchen. These simple 'Jewish ravioli', meaty soup dumplings, are small doughy parcels of salty, fork-tender beef and onion. Sometimes we just need to reach back into our past, to soothe our souls and to warm our bellies with a bowl of rich, golden chicken soup with *kreplach*. — LISA

beef filling
1 litre (4 cups) water
500 g (1 lb 2 oz) gravy (stewing) beef
2 onions, halved and sliced
125 ml (½ cup) oil
½ teaspoon salt
¼ teaspoon white pepper

pasta dough
1 egg
30 ml (1½ tablespoons) oil
1 teaspoon salt
approx 150 ml (scant ⅔ cup) water
425 g (3 cups less 2 tablespoons /15 oz) plain flour, plus extra

to serve
Chicken Soup (page 168)

Start this recipe at least 1 day before serving.

It is easiest to use a pasta machine to roll out the dough. Otherwise, use a rolling pin.

To make the beef filling, put the water in a medium saucepan and bring to the boil over high heat. Add the beef and bring it back to the boil. The water should not be seasoned. Reduce the heat to medium, cover with a lid and simmer for 2 hours. Remove from the heat and allow to cool in the water. Refrigerate (in the water) for at least 24 hours and up to 48.

Sauté the onion in the oil in a medium frying pan over medium-low heat, covered, stirring from time to time, for 1 hour or until well cooked and very dark brown. Allow to cool in the oil. This can be done several days in advance.

When you are ready to make the filling, remove the meat from the fridge. Drain and discard the liquid. Using a mincer, mince the meat with the onion, add the salt and pepper and mix well to combine. Season to taste with extra salt and pepper, as needed. You can also do this in the food processor, but take care not to over process. Refrigerate the filling until needed, for up to 48 hours.

To make the dough, combine the egg, oil and salt in a medium measuring jug. Beat with a fork to combine. Add enough water to reach the 250 ml (1 cup) mark then tip the liquid mixture into the bowl of an electric mixer fitted with a dough hook. Add three-quarters of the flour to the bowl and mix on the lowest speed. Gradually add the remaining flour, until it comes together as a dough, scraping down the sides from time to time. You may not need all of the flour. If, however, the dough is too wet, add a little extra flour until it comes together as a dough. Keep kneading on the lowest speed for 15 minutes or until you have a very smooth and silky dough. The dough can be used immediately or refrigerated for up to 48 hours.

If you are using a pasta machine, clamp your machine to the benchtop. Turn the dial to the widest setting. Divide the dough into 4 pieces and cover each with plastic wrap.

Working with the first piece, flatten it into a rectangle. Sprinkle both sides of the dough with a little flour. Starting with one of the shorter sides of the rectangle, feed it through the rollers. Fold it in half and feed the dough through the machine again, shorter side first, again at the widest setting. If it sticks, sprinkle it with a little more flour. Repeat the folding and rolling a couple of times. Pass the dough through a few more times without folding.

Start to roll it thinner by turning the dial to the next narrowest setting. Feed the dough through and repeat a couple of times (no folding). Reduce the setting to the next narrowest and feed the dough through again. Repeat a couple of times until you have a very smooth sheet, around 3 mm (⅒ in) thick.

You will need a small cup of water for wetting the dough to help it stick, and a lightly floured board.

Lightly flour the benchtop and lay the dough on top. Using a 6.5 cm (2½ in) cookie cutter, cut out circles, leaving as little a gap between the circles as possible. Place a teaspoon (about 10 g/⅓ oz) of filling on a circle. With fingertips, wet the edges of half the circle, fold up to join the two sides of the circle and seal well. Bring the two outer corners together, cross over slightly and press to join. Flip over the top lip, forming a little tortellini-like parcel. Set aside on your lightly floured board. Continue until all the dough and filling has been used.

To cook the *kreplach*, bring a large pot of well-salted water to the boil, with a dash of extra oil. You will need a slotted spoon and a large bowl of cold water. Working in batches, about 12 at a time, add the *kreplach* to the water and stir. Bring the water to the boil again, cover with a lid and simmer for 2 minutes. Stir again and scoop out with the slotted spoon as soon as they float to the surface. Taste to check if the dough is cooked, keeping in mind that you will probably be reheating it later and it will cook a little more.

Place the cooked *kreplach* into the bowl of cold water and repeat with the remaining *kreplach*. Once they are all in the cold water, leave for 5 minutes, then drain the water, cover again with fresh cold water and leave for 5 more minutes. Drain, toss with a drizzle of extra oil and place in one layer in a container. Cover the *kreplach* with a wet paper towel, then seal with plastic wrap or a lid. Refrigerate until ready to serve.

To serve, heat your soup in one pot, and bring another saucepan of salted water to the boil. Slip the desired number of *kreplach* into the salted water and simmer for a few minutes until hot. If you wish to reheat them in the soup, make sure you rinse them in hot water first to remove any oil.

Serve 2–4 **kreplach** *per person with Chicken Soup. Makes about 60* **kreplach**.

TIP: To freeze the cooked *kreplach*, after immersing in cold water and draining, place on a tray, toss with a little oil and spread out so they are not touching. Place in the freezer until frozen solid. They can then be transferred to a plastic bag until needed, at which time they can be reheated from frozen.

SEE IMAGE *page 112.*

SUKKOT + HARVEST

Slow-Cooked Minestrone

In the cooler months we long for a good-to-eat, really healthy, suitable-for-everyone, warming soup. This is it. It is also the perfect vegetable-packed dish for *Sukkot* to celebrate the time of the harvest and its glorious, colourful bounty. — MMCC

2 tablespoons extra-virgin olive oil
1 leek, chopped
2 celery sticks, chopped
2 tablespoons tomato paste
1 teaspoon salt
½ teaspoon ground black pepper
3 carrots, peeled and chopped
3 zucchini, chopped
¼ small green cabbage, chopped
½ bunch Tuscan cabbage (cavolo nero), chopped
2 litres (8 cups) well-flavoured vegetable stock
1 large parmesan rind
400 g (14 oz) tin chickpeas, drained and rinsed well
400 g (14 oz) tin cannellini beans, drained and rinsed well
grated parmigiano reggiano, to serve

It is recommended but not essential to start this recipe the day before so the flavours develop.

Heat the oil in a large stockpot over medium heat. Add the leek and celery and cook for 5 minutes or until slightly softened. Add the tomato paste, salt and pepper and cook for another minute, stirring.

Add the carrot, zucchini, green cabbage, Tuscan cabbage and stock and stir. Add the parmesan rind, bring to the boil, then reduce the heat and simmer, uncovered, for 1 hour 30 minutes.

Add the chickpeas and beans and cook for another hour or until the soup's colour has deepened and the vegetables are soft and sweet. Season to taste.

Serve hot with grated parmigiano reggiano.

Serves 8

Pumpkin, Spinach
and Chickpea Curry

A steaming bowl of a spicy, warming curry is fabulous for a *Sukkot* dinner when the weather outdoors is a bit chilly (no pun intended). So good, so healthy, so bright. To our vegan friends, you're welcome. — MMCC

500 g (1 lb 2 oz) peeled Japanese (Kent) pumpkin, cut into 3 cm (1¼ in) cubes
½ teaspoon ground cinnamon
½ teaspoon ground coriander
1 teaspoon salt
¼ teaspoon ground black pepper
2 tablespoons oil
1 onion, chopped
2 tablespoons curry powder or curry paste
2 x 400 g (14 oz) tins chickpeas, drained and well rinsed
400 ml (1⅔ cups) coconut cream
150 g (5½ oz) baby spinach leaves
juice of 1 lime

to serve
1 red chilli, seeded and sliced
1 small handful fresh coriander leaves or extra fresh spinach leaves
lime wedges
steamed basmati rice

Preheat the oven to 200°C (390°F) conventional.

Toss the pumpkin with the cinnamon, coriander, salt, pepper and 1 tablespoon of the oil in a medium roasting pan. Put in the oven and roast for 20 minutes or until golden brown and just cooked. Set aside.

While the pumpkin is roasting, add the onion to a large, deep frying pan with the remaining oil and sauté over medium heat for 15 minutes, tossing from time to time, or until starting to soften. Add the curry powder or curry paste and cook for a couple of minutes until fragrant. Add the pumpkin and the chickpeas to the pan and toss gently to combine. Add the coconut cream and simmer gently for 10 minutes (do not boil), shaking the pan from time to time. Add the spinach and gently stir. Add salt and pepper to taste, and then the lime juice. Sprinkle with chilli, coriander or extra spinach leaves. Serve with lime wedges to squeeze and rice.

Serves 6

TIP: If you want to use dried chickpeas, soak 250 g (9 oz) in water overnight. Drain, put in a large saucepan with plenty of water and simmer for 45 minutes or until soft. Drain before using. This recipe also works well with large cauliflower florets instead of pumpkin.

Turkish Spiced Snapper

Originally made in a traditional Turkish claypot, this warmly spiced roasted snapper is a pleasure to make, and delivers flavour in spades. We love how it can be prepped in advance, then topped with lemon slices and baked at the last minute. Nowadays we all keep a small jar of Ata's spice blend in the pantry, ready to be sprinkled at a moment's notice. It really is fast food. — MMCC

750 g (1 lb 11 oz/about 4) snapper or other white fish fillets, skin off
1 handful flat-leaf parsley, leaves roughly chopped
50 g (1¾ oz) unsalted butter, chopped
½ teaspoon salt
1 lemon, sliced
1 tablespoon extra-virgin olive oil

Ata's spice blend
2 teaspoons ground turmeric
2 teaspoons ground sweet paprika
2 teaspoons ground hot paprika
2 teaspoons ground cumin
2 teaspoons baharat (Middle Eastern spice mix)
2 teaspoons chilli powder

to serve
steamed rice or Lentil Rice (*majadara*) (page 127)

You will need a wide, flat ovenproof dish.

To make Ata's spice blend, put all the ingredients in a jar and shake to combine.

Toss the fish with 1½ tablespoons of the spice blend (store the rest in the pantry) and three-quarters of the parsley and place in the dish. Dot with the butter. Leave at room temperature for 30 minutes for the flavours to absorb.

Preheat the oven to 210°C (410°F) conventional.

Sprinkle the fish with the salt, top with the lemon slices and drizzle with the olive oil. Cover with foil or a lid and cook for 15 minutes or until the fish flakes at the edges. Remove the foil or lid and return to the oven for 5 minutes or until the fish is just cooked through.

Remove the lemon slices and sprinkle with the remaining parsley leaves. Serve with steamed rice or *majadara*.

Serves 4

Spiced Barbecue Chicken
with Green Hummus and Herb Salad

This dish has three simple components. Each works well on its own but together they create a really fantastic fresh and healthy meal, perfect for al fresco dining any time of the year. It's a dish that will make everyone happy. The vegetarians will be satisfied with loads of chickpeas and abundant greens, while the barbecuer has chicken ready to go. Plus, there's not much washing up as everything can be done ahead of time. – MMCC

spiced chicken
2 tablespoons extra-virgin olive oil
2 teaspoons ground cumin
2 teaspoons ground coriander
2 teaspoons ground cinnamon
1 clove garlic, crushed
8 skinless chicken thigh fillets
1 teaspoon flaky salt

green hummus
120 g (½ cup) tahini
1 clove garlic, roughly chopped
juice of ½ lemon
1½ tablespoons olive oil
60 ml (¼ cup) water
1 heaped cup loosely packed flat-leaf parsley leaves and stems
400 g (14 oz) tin chickpeas, rinsed well and drained
½ teaspoon salt
¼ teaspoon ground black pepper

salad and dressing
1 handful flat-leaf parsley leaves
1 handful mint leaves
1 handful coriander leaves
100 g (3 cups) baby rocket leaves
4 shallots (spring onions), sliced
160 ml (⅔ cup) extra-virgin olive oil
2 tablespoons lemon juice
2 tablespoons apple cider vinegar
½ teaspoon salt
ground black pepper
2 tablespoons slivered almonds, toasted

To make the marinade for the spiced chicken, combine the oil, cumin, coriander, cinnamon and garlic in a small bowl. Rub the spice mixture into the chicken. Refrigerate for at least 30 minutes and up to 24 hours ahead.

To make the hummus, place the tahini, garlic, lemon juice, olive oil and water in a food processor and process until smooth. Add the parsley, chickpeas, salt and pepper and process for a few minutes until very smooth. If it's too thick, add more water. Season to taste with extra salt, pepper and lemon juice, as needed.

To make the salad, roughly chop the herbs and place in a bowl with the rocket and shallot.

To make the dressing, combine the extra-virgin olive oil, lemon juice, apple cider vinegar, salt and a little pepper in a jar. Shake to combine and set aside.

To cook the chicken, sprinkle with the salt. Heat a barbecue or frying pan to hot and cook the chicken for 5 minutes or until a golden crust has formed on the underside. Turn the pieces over, reduce the heat to medium and continue to cook until just cooked through, about 10 minutes. Remove from the heat and leave to rest for 5 minutes.

Just before serving, dress the salad. Shake the jar with the dressing ingredients to remix, then pour over the salad. Toss well and season to taste with extra salt and pepper, as needed. Sprinkle with the toasted slivered almonds.

Serve the three components in separate dishes on the table or spread a large dollop of the green hummus on a platter, arrange the salad on top, then add the chicken pieces and dot with a bit more of the hummus. Drizzle with extra olive oil and serve the rest of the hummus in a bowl alongside.

Serves 4

Stuffed Cabbage Rolls

For me, this dish almost defines comfort food. It takes me straight back to my childhood and to times gone by, sitting and eating hot, tomatoey, cabbage-wrapped parcels of meat and rice in my beautiful Aunty Myrna's tiny kitchen. It is one of those recipes that seems complicated but, once you try it, and get your head around the steps to take, it is really quite straightforward. — LISA

1 whole green cabbage (you will need 8 large leaves)

tomato sauce
2 onions, chopped
60 ml (¼ cup) extra-virgin olive oil
420 g (15 oz) tin condensed tomato soup
800 g (1 lb 12 oz) tomato passata (puree) or diced tomatoes
juice of 1 lemon
1 teaspoon salt
½ teaspoon ground black pepper

beef filling
250 g (9 oz) beef mince
280 g (1½ cups) just-cooked long grain rice (heaped ⅓ cup uncooked)
3 French shallots (eschalots) or 1 onion, finely chopped
½ cup flat-leaf parsley leaves, chopped
2 teaspoons fresh (or 1 teaspoon dried) thyme leaves
1 clove garlic, crushed
1 teaspoon salt
¼ teaspoon ground black pepper

It is recommended but not essential to start this recipe the day before.

Core the cabbage and place in a large pot of cold water so the cabbage is fully submerged. Bring to the boil, cover and simmer for 15 minutes. Remove from the stove and leave to cool in the water. Once cool, drain the water and gently peel off each leaf taking care to not tear it. On the outer leaves, you may need to cut out the thickest part of the stalk to make folding easier.

To make the sauce, fry the onion in the oil in a large, deep frying pan or saucepan over medium-low heat for 20 minutes or until soft and glassy. Add the tomato soup, tomato passata or diced tomatoes, lemon juice, salt and pepper then simmer for 40 minutes. Season to taste with extra salt, pepper and lemon juice, as needed. Set aside.

Put the beef mince in a medium bowl. Add the rice, shallot or onion, parsley, thyme, garlic, salt and pepper. Add 125 ml (½ cup) of the prepared tomato sauce. Mix well and season with extra salt and pepper as needed.

Preheat the oven to 160°C (320°F) conventional. You will need a flameproof casserole dish with a lid, large enough to hold the cabbage rolls snugly in one layer.

Pour the remaining sauce into the casserole dish.

To make the cabbage rolls, lay a cabbage leaf flat on the benchtop. Place approximately 80 g (around ¼ cup) of the meat mixture loosely in a loaf shape in the centre of the leaf. Fold in the sides and then roll it like a parcel. Place the roll into the casserole dish, seam-side down, submerging it as much as possible in the sauce. Repeat with the remaining mixture and cabbage leaves, placing the rolls snugly side-by-side. Any unused or torn leaves can be rolled up and stuffed into the gaps. Make sure all the rolls are covered with sauce.

Place the casserole dish over a medium heat and bring to a light boil, then remove from the heat, cover with the lid (or a double layer of foil) and place in the oven. Cook for 2 hours 30 minutes, basting from time to time. If the cabbage rolls start to dry out, add a little water to ensure they are covered with sauce.

If not serving immediately, leave to cool then cover and refrigerate for up to 3 days.

To serve, reheat for 30 minutes at 160°C (320°F) conventional or until piping hot.

Makes 8 medium-sized cabbage rolls. Serves 4

Pumpkin and Corn Salad
with Tahina

We love making veggies the hero of the *Sukkot* table. This pumpkin and corn salad is not only versatile but also simply gorgeous with its oranges and yellows. Make all the elements a couple of hours ahead and keep at room temperature until serving. – MMCC

1 kg (2 lb 3 oz) Japanese (Kent) pumpkin, skin on
2 teaspoons ground cumin
2 teaspoons ground cinnamon
1 teaspoon brown sugar
salt and ground black pepper
60 ml (¼ cup) extra-virgin olive oil
1 corn cob
100 g (3½ oz) pepitas (pumpkin seeds)
1 small handful coriander leaves, to serve

tahina sauce
100 g (⅓ cup) tahini
juice of ½ lemon
½ clove garlic
¼ teaspoon salt
ground black pepper
100 ml (⅓ cup + 1 tablespoon) water

Preheat the oven to 200°C (390°F) conventional. You will need a lined baking tray.

Cut the pumpkin into chunky pieces. In a small bowl, combine the cumin, cinnamon and sugar and sprinkle over all sides of the pumpkin. Lay the pumpkin on the prepared tray. Season with salt and pepper, drizzle with the oil and roast for 20 minutes until just soft and starting to brown at the edges. The pumpkin should still have a bit of bite if pierced with a knife.

Meanwhile, bring a medium saucepan of salted water to the boil, add the corn cob and cook for 5 minutes. Drain and refresh in cold water. Using a sharp knife, slice down the sides of the cob to remove the kernels, leaving some strips of kernels intact where possible.

Toast the pepitas over medium heat in a dry frying pan for 5 minutes or until they start to pop and turn brown. Remove and set aside.

To make the tahina sauce, combine the tahini, lemon juice, garlic, salt and a little pepper in a bowl and whisk until thick and claggy. Gradually add the water, continuing to whisk until a smooth sauce forms. Season to taste with extra salt, pepper and lemon juice, as needed.

Spread a large dollop of tahina onto a platter. Arrange the pumpkin pieces on top and drizzle with a bit more of the tahina. Top with the corn kernels, toasted pepitas and coriander. Serve the remaining tahina in a bowl alongside.

Serves 8

Lentil Rice
(Majadara)

When we need a side dish that is both hearty and comforting, and works well for a vegan diet, this is the one. It is a perfect blend of aromatic, fluffy basmati rice studded with lentils, gently spiced with cumin and sweetened with caramelised onion. – MMCC

220 g (1 cup/8 oz) basmati rice
310 ml (1¼ cups) water
½ teaspoon salt
60 ml (¼ cup) extra-virgin olive oil
2 onions, halved and finely sliced
2 teaspoons ground cumin
¼ teaspoon ground black pepper
400 g (14 oz) tin brown lentils, rinsed and drained

Put the rice in a sieve and wash under cold running tap water until the water runs clear, then drain.

Put the rice, water and salt in a small saucepan over high heat and bring to the boil, then reduce the heat to low, cover tightly and cook for 10 minutes. Remove the saucepan from the heat and set aside (still covered) for another 10 minutes to finish steaming. Alternatively, use a rice cooker.

Meanwhile, heat the oil in a frying pan over medium heat and sauté the onion for 20 minutes until deep golden brown. Add the cumin and pepper and stir for a minute or until fragrant. Add the lentils to the pan and stir through.

Fluff the rice with a fork. Combine the lentil mixture with the rice and season to taste with extra salt and pepper.

Serve warm.

Serves 6 as a side dish

TIP: This recipe uses tinned lentils. Feel free to substitute ½ cup dried brown lentils, cooked separately until al dente and drained well.

Cauliflower and Sweet Potato Pilaf

Don't be put off by the long list of ingredients in this aromatic rice dish. This is such a regular Friday night dinner dish in my household, particularly if we are having non-meat eaters over. Most of the ingredients can be found in my pantry and I change up the vegetables all the time, depending on what I have on hand. — NATANYA

220 g (1 cup) basmati rice
2 teaspoons garam masala
1 teaspoon ground cumin
½ teaspoon ground turmeric
1½ teaspoons salt
60 ml (¼ cup) oil
300 g (10½ oz) sweet potato, peeled and cut into 2 cm (1 inch) cubes
1 cauliflower, trimmed and cut into florets (approx 800 g/ 1 lb 12 oz)
1 red onion, halved and finely sliced
1 tablespoon grated fresh ginger
2 cloves garlic, crushed
1 tablespoon tomato paste
juice and zest of 1 lemon
1 tablespoon brown sugar
375 ml (1½ cups) vegetable stock
1 cinnamon stick
ground black pepper
115 g (¾ cup) roasted salted cashews
1 small handful fresh coriander leaves

You will need a large, deep frying pan or flameproof casserole with a lid, with a capacity of about 5 litres (20 cups).

Place the rice in a fine-mesh strainer and rinse under cold running water until the water runs clear. Set aside.

Combine the garam masala, cumin, turmeric and salt in a bowl and set aside.

Heat 2 tablespoons of the oil in the casserole over high heat. Add the sweet potato and half the spice mix, and sauté for about 5 minutes or so, tossing regularly, until the edges brown and the sweet potato is partly cooked. Add the cauliflower and cook for a further 5 minutes or so, tossing with the sweet potato, or until the cauliflower starts to soften and brown at the edges. Tip the vegetables into a heatproof bowl and set aside.

Add the remaining oil to the pan and sauté the onion over medium heat for a minute or two. Add the remaining spice mix and cook, stirring, for a minute or until fragrant. Add the ginger, garlic, tomato paste, lemon zest and juice and brown sugar and sauté, stirring, for a minute or so.

Add the rice and mix well, then add the sweet potato and cauliflower. Pour the stock into the pan and add the cinnamon stick. Bring to the boil, cover tightly with a lid and reduce the heat to low. Cook the rice, undisturbed, for 20 minutes. Remove the lid, toss gently with a spoon, season to taste with extra salt and pepper, as needed.

Sprinkle with the cashews and coriander.

Serves 6

Spiced Israeli Couscous with Eggplant

The *mitzvah* (good deed) of eating in a *sukkah* also lends itself to loads of casual, outdoor entertaining. It helps to have an arsenal of recipes that can be easily *shlepped* from the kitchen to the outdoor table. We love that this salad is easy to prep a couple of hours ahead and substantial enough for a meat-free meal. — MMCC

eggplant
1 eggplant
2 teaspoons ground coriander
1 teaspoon salt
60 ml (¼ cup) extra-virgin olive oil

couscous
1 onion, chopped
1 tablespoon extra-virgin olive oil
1 teaspoon ground coriander
¼ teaspoon ground black pepper
250 g (9 oz) Israeli couscous (pearl couscous)
310 ml (1¼ cups) vegetable or chicken stock
1 handful coriander, leaves chopped
1 handful flat-leaf parsley, leaves chopped
1 handful mint, leaves chopped
juice of 1 lemon

Preheat the oven to 150°C (300°F) conventional. Line a baking tray.

Cut the eggplant into 1.5 cm (⅔ in) cubes and place in a large bowl. Sprinkle with the ground coriander, salt and oil and toss until the cubes are roughly coated. Spread onto the tray and roast for 50 minutes or until brown, tossing from time to time to brown evenly. Set aside.

While the eggplant is roasting, make the couscous. In a medium saucepan, sauté the onion in the oil over medium heat for 15 minutes or until soft and golden. Add the ground coriander and black pepper and stir for a minute or until fragrant. Add the couscous and stir until the grains are coated with the spice mix and lightly toasted. Add the stock and bring to the boil. Reduce the heat to very low, cover with a lid and cook for 10 minutes. Toss the couscous with a spatula and scrape the bottom of the pan to loosen any grains that might be stuck. Add extra stock or water if it is looking dry, cover again and cook for another 5 minutes. Remove from the heat, keep covered and allow to steam for a further 5 minutes to finish cooking, then fluff through with a fork to separate the grains.

In a large bowl, mix together the eggplant and the couscous. You can do this ahead of time. When ready to serve, add the herbs and lemon juice and toss. Season to taste. Serve warm or at room temperature.

Serves 6

Broccoli Slaw

In my never-ending quest to load my plate with more green vegetables, I created this crunchy and hearty salad. The mix of raw and roasted broccoli amplifies the flavour, and toasted almonds add extra crunch. I love that it can be made several hours ahead and left on the kitchen counter until it's ready to dress and take outside to the *sukkah*. And while it might not look as zesty and fresh the next day, the leftovers are great, freshened up with a handful of rocket. — **MERELYN**

¼ cup currants
½ red onion, finely sliced
60 ml (¼ cup) white wine vinegar
¼ cup slivered almonds
1 bunch broccolini
2 tablespoons extra-virgin olive oil
1 head broccoli
large handful mint, leaves picked
large handful flat-leaf parsley, leaves picked
handful dill, roughly chopped
salt and ground black pepper
juice of ½ lemon

Preheat the oven to 200°C (390°F) conventional.

Place the currants, onion and vinegar in a small bowl. Stir and set aside.

Place the almonds on a baking tray and bake for 4 minutes or until golden brown. Check them early as they can burn easily. Set aside on a plate to cool.

Chop the broccolini into 2 cm (1 in) pieces. Place on the baking tray used for the almonds (no need to wash), toss with 1 tablespoon of the olive oil, and roast for 5 minutes or until the pieces of stalk are soft and the heads are a bit charred. Set aside to cool.

Cut off the stem of the head of broccoli, trim off the hard skin, then finely julienne or slice. Place in a mixing bowl. Cut the rest of the broccoli into florets, then finely slice each floret. Add to the bowl, along with any little bits that may have fallen off. Add the cooled broccolini, mint, parsley and dill and mix together.

When ready to serve, add the currant and onion mixture and toss. Season to taste with salt and pepper as needed. Mix through the lemon juice and the remaining olive oil. Toss with the roasted slivered almonds just before serving.

Serves 6–8

Pear and Marmalade Cake

Slice through this moist, amazingly dairy-free cake with a beautiful crumb to reveal a hidden layer of pears and marmalade jam. Merelyn's mum, Yolan, originally made this with apples, but it's also delicious when made with any in-season fruit. Plums work beautifully. — MMCC

2 eggs
200 g (1 scant cup/7 oz) caster sugar
180 ml (⅔ cup) oil
1 teaspoon vanilla extract
¼ teaspoon salt
200 g (1⅓ cups/7 oz) self-raising flour, sifted
60 ml (¼ cup) orange juice
2 large pears, peeled and finely sliced
1 tablespoon orange marmalade
1 tablespoon fine cinnamon sugar (see Kitchen Notes, page 13)

Preheat the oven to 180°C (355°F) conventional. Line a 20 cm (8 in) round springform cake tin.

In an electric mixer, beat the eggs and sugar until pale and creamy. Add the oil, vanilla and salt and beat until just combined. Using a spatula, gently fold in half the flour, then the orange juice, followed by the remaining flour.

Pour half the batter into the prepared tin and cover with half the sliced pear. Top with the remaining batter then dot the marmalade on top and cover with the remaining pear slices. Sprinkle with the cinnamon sugar.

Bake for 1 hour or until deep golden and a skewer inserted into the centre comes out clean.

Serves 8

Poppyseed *Beigli* and Walnut *Beigli*

This Hungarian-style rolled pastry has a story to tell of heritage, loss and new beginnings. It's pretty much the story of our people since the beginning of time. These sweet *beigli* have been in my sister-in-law's family for generations, from her maternal grandmother who tragically perished in the Holocaust, to her late mother who started a new life in Sydney and rediscovered the recipe. — LISA

pastry (for two logs)
165 g (1 cup + 1 heaped tablespoon/ 5¾ oz) self-raising flour
85 g (½ cup + 3 teaspoons/3 oz) plain flour
⅛ teaspoon salt
1 teaspoon caster sugar
125 g (4½ oz) unsalted butter, at room temperature
1 egg yolk
75 g (⅓ cup/2¾ oz) sour cream
1½ tablespoons soda water

also needed
2 tablespoons apricot jam
1 egg yolk, beaten, to glaze
icing sugar, to serve

Start this recipe at least 1 day ahead.

To make the pastry, mix together the flours, salt and sugar in a bowl. Rub the butter in with your fingertips until it is spread throughout the flour. In a small bowl, combine the egg yolk and sour cream until smooth. Add to the flour and mix through. Gradually add enough of the soda water until you have a smooth pastry that is not sticky and there is no flour left in the bottom of the bowl. If the mixture is too dry, add a little more soda water.

Divide the pastry into 2 balls. On a floured benchtop, knead each ball for a few minutes with the heel of your hand, back and forth along the benchtop until it is a smooth, silky ball. Wrap each ball in plastic wrap and refrigerate for at least 24 hours.

walnut filling (for two logs)
200 g (2 cups/7 oz) walnuts
or 200 g (1½ cups/7 oz) coarse ground walnuts (walnut meal)
150 g (⅔ cup/5⅓ oz) caster sugar
finely grated zest of ½ lemon
30 g (¼ cup) sultanas
1 egg white

poppyseed filling (for two logs)
150 g (3 cups/5⅓ oz) ground poppy seeds
110 g (½ cup/4 oz) sugar, or to taste
1 teaspoon vanilla extract
30 g (¼ cup) sultanas
250 ml (1 cup) milk
1 egg white

Choose which filling you prefer. Line a baking tray.

To make the walnut filling with whole walnuts, combine the walnuts, sugar and lemon zest in a food processor. Pulse until the walnuts are like coarse breadcrumbs. If using ground walnuts, mix with the sugar and the lemon zest in a small bowl. Using a fork, lightly whisk the egg white until white and frothy, but not stiff. Mix through the walnut mixture and divide the mixture in half.

To make the poppyseed filling, place the poppy seeds, sugar, vanilla, sultanas and milk in a saucepan over medium heat. Cook for 15 minutes, stirring frequently, until it has reduced to become a fairly solid, but still moist, mixture. Allow to cool completely. Using a fork, lightly whisk the egg white until white and frothy, but not stiff, and stir through the poppyseed mixture. Divide the mixture in half.

To make one *beigli* log, remove one ball of pastry from the fridge and leave to come to room temperature. On a lightly floured benchtop, roll out to a thickness of 2 mm (1/16 in) to form a 32 x 22 cm (12 x 8½ in) rectangle. Spread 1 tablespoon of the apricot jam over the pastry from edge to edge, then spread with half of the walnut or poppyseed filling, leaving a 1 cm (½ in) border. Tuck in the ends on the short sides. Roll up the pastry from the long side to form a long log. Place on the prepared tray, seam-side down. Do not flatten. Brush with a little of the beaten egg yolk and, using a fork, prick deeply into the log all along the top. Refrigerate for 20 minutes. Brush once again with the egg and refrigerate for a further 10 minutes. Repeat with the remaining pastry and filling.

Preheat the oven to 180°C (355°F) conventional.

Bake for 35 minutes or until golden. Allow to cool then slice on the diagonal into 1.5 cm (¾ in) wide slices.

To serve, sprinkle with icing sugar.

Each beigli log serves around 8

TIP: The *beigli* pastry often cracks, sometimes along the side and sometimes on the top. It is part of the rustic appeal. Once you slice it, the cracks are hardly noticeable.

SEE IMAGE *page 138.*

Chocolate *Rugelach*

In our many years of searching for the ultimate *rugelach* (Yiddish for 'little twists'), our benchmark has been the yeasted, chocolate-filled miniature crescent pastries found all over Israel. So here's our favourite cream-cheese pastry filled and rolled with buttery chocolate goodness, reminding us of the heartfelt times we've spent with family and friends in our spiritual homeland. – NATANYA

pastry
150 g (1 cup/5⅓ oz) plain flour, plus extra
25 g (1 tablespoon + 1½ teaspoons/ 1 oz) caster sugar
¾ teaspoon baking powder
¼ teaspoon salt
100 g (3½ oz) cold unsalted butter
70 g (2½ oz) cream cheese, room temperature
1 egg yolk
½ teaspoon vanilla extract

filling
40 g (1½ oz) unsalted butter
30 g (1 oz) brown sugar
80 g (2¾ oz) milk chocolate
2 teaspoons unsweetened cocoa powder
pinch of salt

egg wash
1 egg white, lightly beaten

Start this recipe the day before.

To make the pastry, combine the flour, sugar, baking powder and salt in a food processor. Pulse a few times then add the butter and pulse until the mixture resembles breadcrumbs. Add the cream cheese, egg yolk and vanilla and process until the pastry just comes together. Turn the pastry out onto the benchtop and evenly divide into 3 pieces. Wrap each piece in plastic wrap or baking paper and refrigerate overnight.

The next day, prepare the filling. Combine the butter and sugar in a small saucepan over medium heat and cook, stirring, until the sugar is melted. Remove from the heat and add the chocolate, cocoa and salt. Stir gently to combine. Allow to cool to room temperature.

Line a large baking tray.

Working with one piece of pastry at a time, roll out the pastry on a lightly floured benchtop, using a lightly floured rolling pin, into a circle approximately 18 cm (7 in) in diameter. Using an offset spatula, spread one-third of the filling evenly over the pastry. If the filling is too hard, heat gently in the microwave or in a small saucepan to soften slightly. With a sharp knife, cut the circle into 8 equal triangles (or wedges), like a pizza. Roll each triangle, from the wide end to the narrow, into a scroll. Place, pointy-end down, on the prepared tray and gently shape into a crescent. Repeat with the remaining pieces of pastry and filling. Place the tray of *rugelach* in the fridge for at least 20 minutes before cooking.

Meanwhile, preheat the oven to 180°C (355°F) conventional.

Remove the tray from the fridge and, using a pastry brush, brush the egg wash over each *rugelach*. Bake for 20 minutes or until golden.

Makes 24 rugelach

CHAPTER FIVE

Chanukah, Purim, Tu Bishvat

Chanukah and *Purim* both celebrate the survival of the Jewish people at two different times in history.

The festival of light, *Chanukah*, commemorates 'the miracle of the oil' back in the time of the second Jewish temple (around 165 BCE) in Jerusalem after it had been desecrated by King Antiochus IV who had overrun Judea (Israel). A group of Jewish warriors, the Maccabees, fought back to reclaim their homeland. To re-dedicate the Temple, the sacred flame needed to burn continuously, but there was only enough of the ritual oil for one day. Miraculously it lasted for eight, until the oil was able to be replenished. We celebrate by lighting a *chanukiah* (candelabra), starting with one candle and adding one more each night. We spend a joyous week in December eating food fried in oil, celebrating the miracle and our survival. It is a reminder that light will always triumph over darkness.

Fast forward a few months to *Purim* in March.

This is the story of Esther, a heroic and strong Jewish woman. She became queen of Persia and thwarted a plot by Haman, one of the king's advisors, to annihilate the Jewish people. Thanks to her cousin Mordechai's discovery of the evil plan, she convinced the king to spare her people.

We celebrate by sending gifts (*mishloach manot*) and giving charity. We also wear fancy dress at *Purim* parties and eat *hamantashen*, a three-cornered pastry.

In each of these stories, the Jewish people survived an attempted annihilation, which then became a celebration and, in turn, a festival. In true Jewish (food-obsessed) style, food was then created to symbolise the story. In essence, 'they tried to kill us, we survived, let's eat.'

Potato Latkes (page 144).

Potato Latkes

Chanukah is the festival of frying and the number one thing to fry is, without a doubt, the potato. These fat, crisp-edged, soft-centred, roesti-like potato fritters are essential. We all grew up eating latkes but there is a divide. Some eat them sweet with sugar, the Americans can't go past apple sauce and we insist ours are savoury, sometimes with just a sprinkle of salt. — MMCC

600 g (1 lb 5 oz) desiree or floury potatoes
2 eggs, lightly beaten
1 heaped tablespoon plain flour
1 teaspoon salt
ground black pepper
oil, for frying

to serve
crème fraîche
salmon caviar (roe)
flaky salt

Peel and grate the potatoes and immediately place in a colander over a bowl for 15 minutes. Squeeze the grated potato with your hands so that any liquid drains to the bowl below.

Discard any water from the bowl below, keeping the sludge (starch) at the bottom of the bowl. Tip the grated potato into the bowl and toss with the sludge. Add the egg and flour, then season with the salt and pepper, mixing well. Work quickly, it is best to cook the mixture immediately.

Add enough oil to a frying pan to reach a depth of around 5 mm (¼ in) and heat on medium-high until hot (a few strands of potato put in the oil should sizzle straight away). Working in batches, carefully place mounded dessert spoons of the potato mixture into the oil and cook for a few minutes on each side until golden brown. You may need to reduce the heat if they brown too quickly. Drain on a wire rack for a couple of minutes before serving. If cooking ahead of time, do not drain, put them straight onto an oven tray. Reheat in the oven at 180°C (355°F) conventional for 10 minutes or until sizzling.

Serve warm with crème fraîche and salmon caviar (roe). Sprinkle with flaky salt.
Makes 16 latkes

TIP: You can also make one large latke by frying the entire mix in a 24 cm (9 ½ in) frying pan. Cook the first side until really golden and crisp. Flip with two spatulas (or flip it onto a lightweight plate and then slide it back into the pan) and cook until golden. Serve on a platter in the middle of the table, topped with sour cream and Salmon Pastrami (page 54). Tuck in everyone!

Smoked Trout Fish Cakes

I want to call these 'Jewish Fried Fish Cakes'. They have so many elements that feel like Jewish home cooking. My Polish grandfathers both adored fried fish. Crumbed and fried patties, or *cotletten*, a Yiddish word I got from my mum, also feels Jewish. To top it off, the smoked fish and dill shout Jewish deli. And now they are an essential part of our *Chanukah* table, especially when we have had too many latkes and doughnuts. — LISA

200 g (7 oz) hot smoked river trout or other smoked fish, flaked
1 potato, cooked, roughly mashed and cooled to room temperature
¼ cup flat-leaf parsley leaves, chopped
¼ cup dill fronds, chopped
finely grated zest and juice of ½ lemon
3 teaspoons extra-virgin olive oil
½ teaspoon salt
¼ teaspoon ground black pepper
2 tablespoons plain flour
1 egg
90 g (1 cup) panko breadcrumbs
olive oil, for frying
lemon wedges, to serve

To make the fish cakes, combine the smoked trout, potato, parsley, dill, lemon zest and juice, olive oil, salt and pepper in a large bowl. Taste and adjust seasoning with salt, pepper and lemon juice, if needed. Shape the mixture into 8 evenly sized patties.

Put the flour on a plate and season with a little extra salt and pepper. Beat the egg in a separate bowl. Place the breadcrumbs on a separate plate. Arrange them, assembly line style. Place an extra plate alongside. Dip a patty into the flour first, then the egg and then the breadcrumbs, ensuring it is well-coated and re-shaping if necessary. Place on the extra plate. Repeat with the remaining patties.

Add enough oil to a frying pan to reach a depth of around 1 cm (½ in) and heat on medium-high until hot (a few crumbs of mixture put in the oil should sizzle straight away). Working in batches, fry the patties for a few minutes on each side or until golden brown. Reduce the heat if they brown too quickly. Remove and drain on a wire rack.

Serve warm or at room temperature with lemon wedges.

Makes 8 medium fish cakes

Chicken Schnitzel

I have such vivid memories of eating veal schnitzel as a little girl. Once a week, my older brother Mark and I formed a production line with Mum. I started by flouring, Mark would egg and breadcrumb, then Mum would fry. As we got older we were 'promoted' until finally I was trusted to handle the hot oil. That came with the greatest pay off, burning my tongue on schnitzel eaten straight from the pan. The crunch, steam and tender meat is forever seared in my mind. — **MERELYN**

250 g (9 oz) stale sourdough bread with crust removed, or 3 cups sourdough breadcrumbs
500 g (1 lb 2 oz/about 10) chicken tenderloins
40 g (¼ cup) plain flour
¾ teaspoon salt
ground black pepper
2 eggs
oil, for frying
flaky salt and lemon wedges, to serve

To make the breadcrumbs, place the bread in the bowl of a food processor and pulse until you have crumbs. Set aside.

Place one chicken tenderloin on a board. Cover with a piece of baking paper or plastic wrap and, using the flat side of a meat mallet, pound a few times to flatten. Set aside. Repeat with the remaining pieces.

Put the flour on a plate and season with ½ teaspoon of the salt and some pepper. Lightly beat the eggs in a small bowl. Put the breadcrumbs on a separate plate and season with the remaining salt. Arrange them, assembly line style. Place an extra plate alongside.

Dip each piece of chicken, one side at a time, into the flour, shaking off the excess, then dip into the beaten egg, allowing any excess to drip back into the bowl. Lastly, press into the crumbs, coating each side well before transferring onto the extra plate. Refrigerate if not frying within 30 minutes.

To cook the schnitzels, add enough oil to a large frying pan to reach a depth of 1 cm (½ in). Heat the oil on medium-high until hot (a small pinch of breadcrumbs put in the oil should sizzle straight away). Carefully place 2 or 3 schnitzels at a time in the oil, in one layer. Do not crowd the pan – they need to sizzle. Cook for 3 minutes or until golden brown. Peek underneath one of the corners to check the colour. Turn over and cook the other side until golden brown and cooked through.

If the schnitzels brown too quickly, reduce the heat.

Remember that the chicken will continue to cook once you take it out of the oil so take care not to overcook.

Transfer the cooked schnitzels onto a wire rack set over paper towel to catch the drips. Sprinkle with flaky salt to taste.

Eat hot or at room temperature.

Serve with lemon wedges.

Serves 4

TIP: If you prefer the ever popular veal or chicken breast schnitzel, you will need to thinly pound the meat before coating. And if you prefer dry breadcrumbs, simply substitute.

SEE IMAGE *page 148.*

Fried Meatballs,
Tomato Herb Salad and Tahina

My traditional *Chanukah* get-together has always been celebrated at my mum's with three generations of the family. Once the kids were too old for *Chanukah* presents, the focus shifted completely to the food. Every year we do the triple fry: latkes and fried meatballs for mains, followed by doughnuts for dessert. At other times, for a midweek dinner, I make these meatballs larger and finish cooking them in the oven, to serve with a side of fresh tomato salad and a dollop of tahina. — NATANYA

125 g (4 oz) stale sourdough bread with crust removed
500 g (1 lb 2 oz) beef mince
1 egg, beaten
1 onion, grated
1 small handful flat-leaf parsley, leaves finely chopped
2 cloves garlic, crushed
1 teaspoon lemon juice
¼ teaspoon ground paprika
¼ teaspoon ground nutmeg
¼ teaspoon baking powder
2 tablespoons extra-virgin olive oil
salt and ground black pepper
oil, for frying

to serve
Tomato Herb Salad (page 153)
Tahina (page 153)

Put the bread in a large bowl and cover with water for a few minutes. Tip off the water, squeeze the bread well over the sink and grate the bread into the same bowl. Add the beef, egg, onion, parsley, garlic, lemon juice, paprika, nutmeg, baking powder and oil. Mix with your hands to combine. Season generously with salt and pepper and combine well.

In a deep frying pan, add enough oil to reach a depth of about 3 cm (1¼ in) and heat on medium-high until hot (a small pinch of meatball mixture put in the oil should sizzle straight away). Prepare a small bowl with water. With wet hands, shape the mixture into small meatballs, about the size of a large walnut. Working in batches, fry for about 5 minutes, turning regularly and reducing the heat if they brown too quickly. Check one of the meatballs to see if it is cooked through and cook for longer, at a lower temperature, if needed.

Serve with Tomato Herb Salad and Tahina.

Makes about 20 meatballs

SEE IMAGE *page 152.*

Tomato Herb Salad

500 g (1 lb 2 oz) cherry tomatoes
4 ripe roma tomatoes
½ teaspoon salt
1 small handful flat-leaf parsley, leaves roughly chopped
1 small handful mint, leaves roughly chopped
1 small handful fresh oregano, leaves roughly chopped
½ red onion, finely sliced
80 ml (⅓ cup) extra-virgin olive oil
2 tablespoons red wine vinegar
ground black pepper

Halve the cherry tomatoes and thickly slice the roma tomatoes. Sprinkle with the salt and leave for 30 minutes. Drain off any excess water and put the tomato in a bowl. Add the herbs and onion and toss gently. Add the olive oil and vinegar, a good pinch of salt and grind of pepper and toss. Season to taste again if needed and serve.

Serves 6

Tahina

100 g (⅓ cup) tahini
juice of ½ lemon
½ clove garlic
¼ teaspoon salt
ground black pepper
100 ml (⅓ cup + 1 tablespoon) water

To make the tahina, combine the tahini, lemon juice, garlic, salt and a little pepper in a bowl and whisk until thick and claggy. Gradually add the water, continuing to whisk until a smooth sauce forms. Season to taste with extra salt, pepper and lemon juice, as needed.

Israeli Salad
with Farro and Chickpeas

The minor festival of *Tu Bishvat*, which celebrates the birthday of trees, has become more popular in recent years reflecting our community's sensitivity to, and appreciation of, the environment. It is customary to eat the 'seven species of fruits' – pomegranate, grapes, dates, figs, olives, wheat and barley – during this festival. This substantial dish showcases farro, a wheat grain, alongside a colourful and well-textured 'Israeli-style' salad that truly celebrates the best of the harvest. – MMCC

200 g (1 cup) roasted farro
400 g tin (1½ cups) chickpeas, drained and rinsed
2 tablespoons extra-virgin olive oil, plus extra
100 g (4 cups) baby rocket leaves
200 g (1 heaped cup) cherry tomatoes, halved
3 Lebanese cucumbers, thickly sliced
2 shallots (spring onions), sliced
200 g (8 oz) feta
salt and ground black pepper

za'atar
2 teaspoons ground sumac
3 teaspoons dried thyme
2 teaspoons dried oregano
3 teaspoons toasted sesame seeds
½ teaspoon salt

dressing
2 tablespoons lemon juice
80 ml (⅓ cup) extra-virgin olive oil
½ teaspoon salt
ground black pepper

Bring a large saucepan of salted water to the boil. Add the farro and return to the boil, reduce the heat and simmer for 40 minutes or until tender. Drain and set aside.

Meanwhile, preheat the oven to 250°C (480°F) conventional.

Toss the chickpeas with the olive oil and spread on a baking tray. Place in the oven and roast for 20 minutes or until golden brown and crunchy, tossing occasionally. Take care as they will splatter.

To make the za'atar, combine the sumac, thyme, oregano, sesame seeds and salt in a bowl. Once the chickpeas are roasted, remove from the oven and add 1 tablespoon of the za'atar, tossing to coat well. Set aside.

To make the dressing, combine the lemon juice, oil, salt and a little pepper in a small jar or bowl and shake or whisk to combine.

Combine the farro, rocket, tomato, cucumber and shallot in a large bowl. Just before serving, add the dressing and toss well, then season to taste with extra salt and pepper as needed.

Top with the feta and chickpeas. Drizzle with the extra oil and sprinkle with a little extra za'atar to serve.

Serves 6

Cinnamon Doughnuts
(Sufganiot)

Hot doughnuts always remind me of Sunday mornings with my dad, down at Port Melbourne looking at the ships. Without fail, we would buy a bag of the most delicious jam doughnuts from the nearby doughnut truck. I don't ever remember seeing a ship, but I do remember the feeling of biting into the super-hot doughy morsel, coating my lips in sugar and burning my tongue on the jam inside.

This recipe for cinnamon-sugared doughnuts (sorry, no jam in these!) needs very little effort. The make-ahead batter is just spooned into the hot oil, tossed in cinnamon sugar and fed to your very happy people. – LISA

300 g (2 cups/10½ oz) bread flour
1 tablespoon caster sugar
10 g (1½ sachets/3 teaspoons) dried yeast
½ teaspoon salt
125 ml (½ cup) milk
1 egg
70 ml (3½ tablespoons) vegetable oil
250 ml (1 cup) water

coarse cinnamon sugar
1½ cups white sugar
3 teaspoons ground cinnamon

also needed
oil, for frying

Combine the flour, sugar, yeast and salt in the bowl of an electric mixer. Whisk for 30 seconds to combine. Add the milk, egg, oil and water and whisk on low speed to combine, then increase the speed to medium-high and continue to whisk for 5 minutes or until the mixture is glutinous (a little stretchy) and shiny.

Leave to stand at room temperature for 1 hour, or up to several hours in the fridge, to allow the mixture to rise. Meanwhile, make the cinnamon sugar by combining the sugar and cinnamon in a wide bowl.

To cook the doughnuts, pour enough oil into a medium saucepan to a depth of at least 10 cm (4 in). Heat on medium heat until a cook's thermometer reads 170°C (340°F) or until a cube of bread dropped in the oil turns golden brown in 20–25 seconds. You can also use a deep fryer. Use 2 dessert spoons to shape the doughnut: one to scoop the mixture out of the bowl, one to scrape it into the hot oil.

Working in batches of around 3–4 doughnuts at a time, so as to not crowd the pan, scoop dessert-spoonfuls of batter into the oil and cook for around 2 minutes or until golden brown, then gently flip using a fork and continue to cook. When golden brown on the second side, remove with a slotted spoon and set aside on a wire rack placed over some paper towel to catch the drips. Toss in the cinnamon sugar.

Serve immediately.
Makes 18–20 doughnuts

TIP: It's easiest if you have a deep fryer or use a cook's thermometer when frying. These doughnuts are best fried in oil at 170°C (340°F). It's a good idea to try one from your first batch to check if the oil temperature is correct; the doughnut should be golden brown on the outside and cooked through in the middle.

Hamantashen
Three Ways

During *Purim*, we celebrate the survival of the Jewish people (see the story, page 143) by eating three-cornered pastries that represent the evil Haman's three-cornered hat. We pretty much turned the villain into a pastry. These beautifully biscuity *hamantashen* will, without a doubt, become part of your annual *Purim* repertoire. They are sweet enough for the kids and not too sweet for the adults – and we have three different fillings to ensure everyone is satisfied. – MMCC

pastry
200 g (7 oz) unsalted butter, at room temperature
50 g (⅓ cup + 3 teaspoons/1¾ oz) icing sugar
⅛ teaspoon salt
1 egg, lightly beaten
½ teaspoon vanilla extract
150 g (1 cup/5⅓ oz) plain flour, plus extra
150 g (1 cup/5⅓ oz) self-raising flour

fillings (see page, far right)
thick raspberry + vanilla jam
nutella + halva
'stuffed monkey' (dried fruit + jam)

eggwash
1 egg, lightly beaten with 1 tablespoon water

Line a large baking tray.

In the bowl of an electric mixer, beat together the butter, icing sugar and salt for a few minutes until well combined. Add the egg and vanilla and beat to combine.

In a separate bowl, mix the flours together. On low speed, add the flour to the butter mixture, one-quarter at a time. Once a soft dough has formed, remove from the mixer bowl and shape into a flat disc. Wrap in plastic wrap and refrigerate for at least 30 minutes.

Divide the dough into 4 pieces. Each piece will make about 10 *hamantashen*. On a well-floured benchtop, using a lightly floured rolling pin, roll out 1 piece of the dough to a thickness of 3 mm (⅒ in). Using a 7 cm (2¾ in) cookie cutter, cut out circles. Place ½–1 teaspoon of your chosen filling (see options, right) in the centre of each circle.

Fold the *hamantashen* by folding three flaps as follows:
Take the left side of the circle and fold it towards the centre so it covers the left third of the circle.
Take the upper right side of the circle and fold it towards the middle, overlapping the previous flap at the top, creating a triangular tip. You will see a small triangle of filling in the middle.
Take the bottom edge of the circle and fold it up towards the top to complete the triangle. When you fold this part up, tuck the left side of this flap underneath the bottom of the first (left) flap you folded, and let the right side of this flap overlap the second flap you folded.
Gently pinch each corner to secure and place on the prepared tray.

Re-roll the scraps, fill and fold as above.
Refrigerate for at least 30 minutes before baking. Preheat the oven to 180°C (355°F) conventional. Brush each *hamantashen* with egg wash. Bake for 15 minutes or until light golden.
Makes about 40 **hamantashen.** *Store in an airtight container for up to 2 weeks.*

SEE IMAGE *page 160.*

CHANUKAH, PURIM, TU BISHVAT

Thick Raspberry and Vanilla Jam Filling

375 g (1 cup) raspberry jam
½ teaspoon vanilla extract

Spoon the jam into a small saucepan and bring to the boil over medium heat, stirring from time to time. Reduce the heat to medium-low and simmer for 10 minutes or until the mixture has reduced by about one-sixth (to 200 ml/⅘ cup). Take care, the jam is very hot. Set aside to cool. Once it cools a little, stir in the vanilla then pour it back into the original jam jar and allow to cool completely. Use ½–¾ teaspoon in each *hamantashen*. Filling will keep refrigerated for about 3–6 months.
Makes enough for at least 48 hamantashen

Nutella and Halva Filling

70 g (¼ cup) Nutella or chocolate hazelnut spread
40 g (¼ cup) halva, finely shaved

In a small bowl with a wooden spoon, mix together the Nutella and halva. It's not essential, but if you refrigerate the filling for at least 30 minutes before using, it is easier to use. Use ¾–1 teaspoon filling in each *hamantashen*.
Makes enough for at least 24 hamantashen

'Stuffed Monkey' Filling

40 g (¼ cup) apricot jam
6 Australian or Californian (not Turkish) dried apricots
1 tablespoon currants
1 tablespoon sultanas
1 tablespoon raisins
½ teaspoon ground cinnamon

Place all the filling ingredients on a large chopping board and, using a large knife, chop the dried fruit with the jam until you have a rough paste. You can also do this in a mini food processor. Use ¾–1 teaspoon filling in each *hamantashen*.
Makes enough for 24 hamantashen

CHAPTER SIX

Pesach

PASSOVER

Passover, or *Pesach*, is the time we want our *Matzo* Balls (page 169) to taste just like our mother's (or in Merelyn's case, just like her dad's), we make Fried *Gefilte* Fish (page 80) by hand, we agonise over how many briskets we need to feed our ever-expanding families. We all grapple with how to squeeze in just one more chair around the table, when the legs are already overlapping.

It is without doubt – food wise – the most complicated and challenging of festivals yet ultimately brings the most joy through the feasts and freedom associated with it. *Pesach* celebrates the Exodus, when Moses saved the Israelites from slavery in Egypt (around 1313 BCE) and guided them through the desert back to their ancestral homeland. For eight days in March or April (seven in Israel), we replace bread with *matzo*, a specially crafted cracker, to remember how the Israelites fled without enough time for their bread to rise. And so, even though *matzo* is made from flour, generally speaking we abstain from all other foods made from wheat (and other grains) that swell or rise. People from different backgrounds have different rules for *Pesach*. Some will avoid rice and, others, peas and lentils. It's a time when Ashkenazis might look longingly at the Sephardi kitchen and wish for their ingredient list.

We celebrate by feasting and by reading the *Haggadah* (a special book of stories, prayers and songs) at the *Pesach* dinner, the *seder*.

This meal is laden with tradition and ritual. Often lasting long into the night, the *seder* is full of questions and answers involving the whole family from young to old, to retell the story of freedom from one generation to the next. Children wait hungrily for dinner. The youngest at the table, sometimes reluctantly, sings *ma nishtana*, 'why is this night different to all other nights?'. We all used to be the youngest at the table, dreading the moment we had to sing, and now can't wait for the joy when our grandchildren continue the tradition.

There is always a '*seder* plate' set out with six symbolic foods to represent the hardships suffered by the slaves. *Zeroah* (roasted shank bone – actually, we often use a chicken wing), *karpas* (parsley), *chazeret* (bitter herbs – cos lettuce), *maror* (horseradish), *beitzah* (roasted egg) and *charoset* (apple and nut paste, page 166), with the *matzo* alongside. We also have salted water for dipping, to remind us of the tears cried in slavery. Throughout the course of the meal, we say blessings over – and drink – four cups of wine, to acknowledge, among other things, the shift from slavery to freedom.

Seder plate, Apple (Ashkenazi) Charoset
(page 166) and *matzo*.

Over the eight days of *Pesach*, there is a common lament, 'What's to eat?' Not pasta, not pizza, no bread, no flour, lots of *matzo*. We combine traditional (*Matzo* Brei, page 180) with new and inventive (*Charoset* Ice cream Parfait, page 185) dishes to compensate for our somewhat limited pantry.

Recipes in this chapter are our family go-tos; you'll find loads of other KLP (kosher for Passover) recipes throughout the book.

It's a haunting and heartwarming feeling to know that around the world, almost all Jewish people are sitting at their *seder* tables, all remembering and valuing their freedom.

At the end of the meal, we all recite the final line from the *Haggadah*, 'Next Year in Jerusalem', reflecting the wishes of an exiled people to return to their homeland.

Charoset

Charoset is a symbolic food universally enjoyed at the *Pesach seder*. It is a mixture of apples and nuts, sweetened with honey, wine or dates, and is one of the six items on the ritual *seder* plate alongside *matzo*. It is an unlikely pairing to say a delicious spread reminds us of the mortar used by the Israelites when they were slaves in Egypt, but it also reminds us that through all the bitterness there are moments of sweetness.

The battle between Ashkenazi and Sephardi recipes continues here. The first is Lisa's family recipe, a traditional Ashkenazi version. The second is Merelyn's with a Sephardi twist. After the *seder*, both are excellent spread on *matzo* for breakfast. – MMCC

Apple (Ashkenazi) *Charoset*

2 Granny Smith apples, peeled
75 g (¾ cup) walnuts
1½ teaspoons ground cinnamon
2 tablespoons honey
2 tablespoons sweet Passover wine or port

Using a box grater, coarsely grate the apples into a medium bowl. Coarsely chop the walnuts and add to the bowl, along with the cinnamon, honey and wine or port. Mix well and allow to sit for 10 minutes. Adjust with more cinnamon, honey or wine or port to your liking. Store in the fridge for up to 4 days.
Makes about 2 cups.

Date (Sephardi) *Charoset*

150 g (1 cup) medjool dates, pitted and chopped
1 Granny Smith apple, peeled and chopped
60 ml (¼ cup) water
160 g (1⅔ cup) walnuts, chopped
115 g (⅓ cup) silan (date molasses)
1½ teaspoons ground cinnamon
finely grated zest of ½ orange
pinch of salt

In a small saucepan over medium heat, combine the date, apple and water. Cook, covered and stirring from time to time, for about 15 minutes until soft. Allow to cool slightly.

Add the walnut, silan, cinnamon, orange zest and salt and mix together until the mixture turns into a rough spread. Taste the mixture and add extra silan or cinnamon as needed. Store in the fridge for up to 2 weeks.
Makes 2 cups.

Chicken Soup and *Matzo* Balls

It is a universally accepted truth that Jewish-style chicken soup is pretty much penicillin. And not only is it good for the constitution, it also nourishes the soul. This is the simplest chicken soup we have come across and it is full of amazing flavour. This is a clear, rich soup which jellies when cold. Best served piping hot with *Matzo* Balls (far right) or after *Pesach* with *Kreplach* (page 110). — MMCC

Chicken Soup

1.5 kg (3 lb 5 oz) chicken frames (carcass)
1 kg (2 lb 2 oz) chicken wings
1 kg (2 lb 2 oz) chicken drumsticks
4.5 litres (18 cups) water
2 carrots, peeled and quartered
1 large onion, unpeeled and quartered
3 sprigs dill
3 stalks parsley
1 tablespoon whole black peppercorns
1 tablespoon salt (see TIP)

Start this recipe the day before serving.

Place the chicken frames, wings, drumsticks and water in an extra-large stockpot. Place over high heat and bring to the boil. When it comes to the boil, a scum will form on top. Skim off and discard. Add the carrot, onion, dill, parsley, peppercorns and salt. Bring to the boil again. Reduce the heat to low, partially cover with a lid and continue to cook at a light boil for 2 hours.

Leave to cool for 30 minutes before straining the soup into a large bowl, discarding all solid ingredients except the meat from the chicken drumsticks and the carrot. Put the chicken meat and carrot in a separate bowl, and cover and refrigerate until needed. Season the soup with extra salt and pepper, as needed (see TIP). Leave to cool and refrigerate overnight. The next day, skim off the fat from the surface. You can freeze the fat (*schmaltz*) for later use.

To serve, reheat the soup by bringing to the boil and simmering for a few minutes. Serve with the carrots and reserved chicken meat if you wish.

Serve within 3 days or freeze for future use.

Makes about 4 litres (16 cups)

TIP: If you use kosher chickens, you will need to add less salt than the recipe directs. Taste for seasoning once cooked, adding extra salt and pepper as needed. If the flavour is not strong enough, simmer and reduce over medium heat until just right. This recipe makes a huge quantity of soup. If it is more than you need, freeze it for another day.

Matzo Balls

Matzo ball soup is perhaps the most quintessential and iconic Ashkenazi Jewish dish. Everyone thinks their mother's, grandmother's or aunty's *matzo* balls are the best. This recipe may challenge your opinion. Whether you like them hard or soft, cooked in the soup or not, made ahead and frozen or not, *matzo* balls are simply the most delicious, soul-soothing soup dumplings. As our spoons slice through the first *matzo* ball, we are immediately and deeply connected to generations past. — MMCC

3 eggs, separated
¾ teaspoon salt
125 g (1 cup/4½ oz) coarse *matzo* meal (see TIP)
60 ml (¼ cup) oil or melted *schmaltz* (see Kitchen Notes, page 13)
60 ml (¼ cup) water
⅛ teaspoon ground black pepper

Using an electric mixer, whisk the egg whites and salt on medium speed until stiff peaks form.

Meanwhile in a separate bowl, with a fork, combine the egg yolks, *matzo* meal, oil or *schmaltz*, water and pepper. While continuing to whisk the egg whites on a low speed, add the *matzo* meal mixture, spoon by spoon, into the whites, whisking to combine after each addition. Set aside for 15 minutes, giving it a light fold halfway through. The mixture will be the texture of stiff porridge, and you should be able to shape a small ball with your hands.

In the meantime, bring a large saucepan of well-salted water to the boil. With wet hands, and without pressing too firmly, lightly roll the *matzo* ball mixture into smooth walnut-sized balls and drop into the boiling water. After the last ball has been dropped in, cover, turn the heat to medium and simmer rapidly for 40 minutes. Remove the pot from the heat and allow the balls to cool in the water.

Refrigerate in the cooking liquid for up to 3 days until ready to use. When ready to serve, remove with a slotted spoon and reheat in the chicken soup.

Serve 2–3 balls per person. Makes about 20 balls.

TIP: The quality of *matzo* meal has changed over the years. This recipe works best with pure coarse *matzo* meal, so if the packet you bought has lots of finer 'sandy' *matzo* meal in it, you will need to tip it into a sieve and remove the fine meal before measuring. Save the fine meal for crumbing your schnitzels (page 150) or for your *ulnyik* (page 178). *Matzo* meal is widely available in kosher food stores and in some supermarkets in the weeks before *Pesach*.

SEE IMAGE *page 165.*

Fish with Roasted Cherry Tomatoes

Here's a quick dinner for two that is so good, so light and a welcome relief from all the serious *fressing* you've been doing during *Pesach*. A one-step Italian-style, roasted tomato sauce with a piece of lovely fresh white fish to soak up all that flavour. It's a definite new favourite. — MMCC

650 g (1 lb 7 oz) multi-coloured cherry tomatoes
1 red onion, sliced
50 g (⅓ cup) pitted kalamata olives
4 anchovies, roughly chopped
1 tablespoon salted capers, rinsed and drained
1 clove garlic, finely sliced
60 ml (¼ cup) extra-virgin olive oil, plus extra
salt and ground black pepper
400 g (14 oz) white fish fillets (such as snapper), skinned and deboned

Preheat the oven to 220°C (428°F) conventional.

Halve any larger cherry tomatoes (the smaller ones can stay whole). Put the tomatoes, onion, olives, anchovies, capers and garlic in a large, deep ovenproof frying or small roasting pan. Drizzle the oil over the top. Roast, uncovered, for 30 minutes, tossing from time to time, or until soft and a little caramelised, but not so much that all of the liquid has evaporated. Season to taste with salt and pepper.

Meanwhile, season the fish with salt and pepper. When the sauce is done, remove it from the oven and place the fish fillets on top, burying them a little in the sauce. Drizzle with a little extra oil and roast for 10 minutes for thinner fillets or up to 15 minutes for thicker fillets, or until just cooked through.

Serves 2–3

Traybake Chicken
with Zucchini and Fennel

I love that this is equally great for the *seder* table or a quick midweek meal all year round. It is one of my family's favourite chicken traybakes. Incredibly simple to assemble, the roasted olives and crunchy capers on top of the chicken dial the umami factor right up. Finger-licking good! – **MERELYN**

3 large zucchini, sliced into rounds
1 large fennel, trimmed and cut into 8 wedges
2 cloves garlic, unpeeled
6 chicken thigh cutlets (skin on, bone in)
250 ml (1 cup) white wine
¼ teaspoon salt
¼ teaspoon ground black pepper
75 g (½ cup) pitted kalamata olives, halved
50 g (¼ cup) capers, rinsed and drained
1 tablespoon extra-virgin olive oil
3 thyme sprigs

Preheat the oven to 200°C (390°F) conventional. Grease a roasting pan.

Place the zucchini, fennel and garlic in the pan, then top with the chicken pieces. Pour the wine over the chicken then season with salt and pepper. Scatter the olives and capers on top, trying to balance some of them directly on top of the chicken. Pour the olive oil over the chicken, then scatter with thyme.

Roast for 50 minutes or until the chicken is golden and the juices run clear when pierced with a knife. If the chicken is not browned enough, turn the oven to the hottest setting for the last 5 minutes.

Serves 4

Greek-Style, Slow-Cooked Lamb

Set and forget. For the frantic lead up to *seder* night, here is a simple, yet completely fabulous, Greek-style, slow-cooked lamb. Marinate the day before, then slow cook while time runs away with all the other last-minute things to do. The result is a platter of tender pulled lamb, prettily strewn with fragrant fresh herbs and onion. Presto. — MERELYN

1 lamb shoulder, on the bone
180 ml (¾ cup) water

marinade
1 tablespoon dried oregano
¼ cup fresh oregano leaves, chopped
2 cloves garlic, chopped
finely grated zest of 1 lemon
juice of ½ lemon
2 tablespoons extra-virgin olive oil
½ teaspoon salt
¼ teaspoon ground black pepper

to serve
juice of ½ lemon
1 handful flat-leaf parsley, leaves roughly chopped
1 handful mint, leaves roughly chopped
½ red onion, sliced
1 lemon, cut in wedges

This recipe is best started the day before serving.

To make the marinade, in a small bowl, mix together the dried oregano, fresh oregano, garlic, lemon zest and juice, olive oil, salt and pepper. Place the lamb in a large dish and massage the marinade into the meat. Cover and refrigerate overnight.

Take the lamb out of the fridge 1 hour before cooking. Preheat the oven to 140°C (285°F) conventional. Place the lamb in a roasting pan. Add the water, cover tightly with foil to completely seal, and roast for 2 hours. Reduce the temperature to 110°C (230°F) conventional and cook for a further 4 hours. Remove the foil, baste with the pan juices and continue to cook, uncovered, for another 1 hour until dark brown and falling off the bone.

Remove from the oven and leave the lamb to cool slightly, then pull the lamb from the bone into large shards. Place on a platter and drizzle with the lemon juice, then garnish with the parsley, mint, red onion and lemon wedges to serve.

Serves 4–6

TIP: Plan ahead – this lamb dish needs at least a day or night to marinate followed by 7 hours in the oven. If you can't find fresh oregano, use parsley.

Red Wine Brisket

In our years of brisket eating, we found a desperate need for a simple, savoury (rather than the usual sweet), slow-cooked recipe. This is it. Our Red Wine Brisket is inspired by a wonderful Slow-Cooked Pepper Beef Ragu in Elizabeth Hewson's *Saturday Night Pasta* (Plum/Pan Macmillan, 2020). The original had loads of garlic and six anchovy fillets, which we've left out, as we know they don't work for everyone. — MMCC

½ teaspoon salt
1 teaspoon ground black pepper
1 x 1.4 kg (3 lb 2 oz) piece beef brisket
2 tablespoons extra-virgin olive oil
2 cloves garlic, crushed
125 ml (½ cup) tomato paste
250 ml (1 cup) red wine
2 rosemary sprigs
500 ml (2 cups) beef or chicken stock
60 ml (¼ cup) balsamic vinegar

to serve
Potato *Ulnyik* (page 178)

Start this recipe 1 day ahead.

Preheat the oven to 130°C (266°F) conventional. You will need a flameproof casserole dish with a lid or a roasting pan.

Combine the salt and pepper and rub all over the brisket.

Heat the oil in the casserole dish over medium heat. Sear the brisket for a few minutes on each side until well browned. Remove the brisket from the casserole dish and set aside.

Add the garlic and tomato paste and cook for a minute or so, stirring. Add the red wine and rosemary, bring to the boil and continue to boil for about a minute. Add the stock and balsamic vinegar and return the brisket to the casserole dish. The liquid should almost cover the brisket. If not, add a little more stock. Bring the liquid back to the boil, cover the brisket with a piece of baking paper and then the lid or, if using a roasting pan, a double layer of foil, tightly sealed. Place in the oven and cook for 3 hours. If it is completely fork tender (check a few places on the brisket), it is ready. If not, cook for an additional 30 minutes or until fork tender. Remove from the oven, uncover and allow to cool slightly.

Remove the brisket from the sauce and set aside. Place the casserole dish on the stove and, over medium heat, bring the sauce to the boil and continue to cook for 20 minutes or until reduced by about one-third. Taste for seasoning. Return the brisket to the sauce, allow to cool and then refrigerate overnight.

The next day, about 90 minutes before serving, take the casserole dish out of the fridge. Remove and discard any fat that has formed on top.

Preheat the oven to 180°C (355°F) conventional. Finish cooking the brisket, uncovered, for 1 hour or until sizzling and glazed, basting from time to time. Slice the brisket thickly across the grain (see TIP on page 90) to serve. (You may find it more convenient to slice the meat before the final hour of cooking.)

Serve with Potato *Ulnyik*.
Serves 6

TIP: Our brisket cooking time rule is 1 hour at 130°C (266°F) conventional for every 450 g (1 lb) of brisket, plus an extra 1 hour at 180°C (355°F) conventional to serve. It is always better cooked the day before and reheated. See *Rosh Hashanah* Brisket (page 90) for important brisket info.

Potato *Ulnyik*

For more than 50 years, my parents hosted the *Pesach seder*. The menu was identical every single year; that is what we call tradition. My mum always made 'Paula's calf brisket', a slow-cooked, onion-smothered, succulent brisket on the bone, but the highlight was always, without a doubt, the accompanying *ulnyik*, an oven-tray size slab of golden fried, salty, oily potato *roesti*. You can find the brisket recipe in our first book, *Monday Morning Cooking Club*. — LISA

125 ml (½ cup) oil
1 kg (2 lb 3 oz) (about 4 large) desiree or floury potatoes
1 onion
1 egg, lightly beaten
½ teaspoon salt
¼ teaspoon ground black pepper
2 tablespoons fine *matzo* meal or plain flour

Preheat the oven to 200°C (390°F) conventional. Line the base of a shallow roasting pan (approx 32 x 23 x 3 cm/12 x 9 x 1¼ in).

Pour the oil into the pan and place in the oven as it preheats.

Using the coarse side of a box grater or a food processor with a large-hole grating attachment, grate the potatoes and onion. Place in a large colander over a bowl and leave for 10 minutes. Squeeze any additional liquid out of the potato with your hands. Discard the liquid from the bowl, keeping any starchy sludge that has settled at the bottom. Place the potato into the bowl. Add the egg, salt, pepper and *matzo* meal or flour and mix well, including the sludge.

Remove the hot pan from the oven, and carefully (it's hot!) spoon the potato mixture into the pan. Smooth the mixture out so it is evenly spread from corner-to-corner and edge-to-edge, without pressing down too much.

Cook for 1 hour or until golden brown.

If serving later, leave to cool, remove from the tin and cut into 8 or 10 pieces. Reheat in an oven at 180°C (355°F) conventional for 20 minutes or until crisp and sizzling.

Serves 8

TIP: It is not essential but this recipe works well made a few hours or even a couple of days ahead. It is easier to slice when cool and reheats very well.

Matzo Brei

At *Pesach* time, when many of us are desperately missing bread, we need to create dishes to fill the void. The simplest thing to make is a quick *matzo* brei. Here are two versions. The first is the basic recipe and can be served savoury with salt and sour cream or sweet with cinnamon sugar. The second is a more substantial dish with leek, mushrooms and feta. – MMCC

Basic *Matzo* Brei

4 pieces *matzo*
2 eggs
60 ml (¼ cup) milk
½ teaspoon salt
1 tablespoon butter
sour cream and salt or cinnamon sugar (see Kitchen Notes, page 13), to serve

Break the *matzo* into 2 cm (¾ in) pieces and place in a bowl. Cover with tap water and soak for 5 minutes. Drain in a colander and squeeze out the excess water. In a medium bowl, beat the eggs with the milk and salt. Add the *matzo* and stir to combine.

Heat a medium frying pan over high heat and add the butter. Heat until melted and sizzling, then add the *matzo* mixture. Reduce the heat to medium-high and cook for a few minutes. Once the bottom sets, toss the mixture around in the pan. Let it set again for a minute and repeat until it is cooked through. Serve with sour cream and salt or cinnamon sugar, as you wish.

Serves 2–4

Leek and Mushroom *Matzo* Brei

4 pieces *matzo*
2 eggs
60 ml (¼ cup) milk
½ teaspoon salt
1 small leek, white only, finely sliced
2 teaspoons extra-virgin olive oil
2 tablespoons butter
4 large button mushrooms, sliced
¼ teaspoon salt
⅛ teaspoon ground black pepper
1 large handful baby spinach leaves
100 g (3½ oz) feta, roughly chopped
1 shallot (spring onion), to serve

Break the *matzo* into 2 cm (¾ in) pieces and place in a bowl. Cover with tap water and soak for 5 minutes. Drain in a colander and squeeze out the excess water. In a medium bowl, beat the eggs with the milk and salt. Add the *matzo* and stir to combine. Set aside.

In a medium frying pan over medium heat, sauté the leek in the oil and half the butter until starting to soften. Add the mushroom, salt and pepper and cook, tossing from time to time, until softened. Add the spinach, toss quickly, remove from the pan and set aside.

Return the pan to the heat and add the remaining butter. Heat until melted and sizzling, then add the *matzo* mixture. Reduce the heat to medium-high and cook for a few minutes. Once the bottom sets, toss the mixture around in the pan. Let it set again for a minute and repeat until it is cooked through. Just before it is cooked through, stir through the feta. Top with the leek mixture and sprinkle with shallot to serve.

Serves 2–4

Roasted Apple *Matzo* Kugel

In our grandmothers' day, *matzo* kugel ruled the *Pesach* dessert table, alongside nut cake and fruit compote. This warm, sweet, fragrant pudding delivers all the happiness of a bread-and-butter pudding with all the *nachas* (unbridled joy) of 'keeping *Pesach*' (refraining from eating all those prohibited foods for a whole eight days). – MMCC

roasted apples
3 Granny Smith (or other baking) apples, peeled and finely sliced
1 tablespoon apple cider vinegar or water
1 tablespoon butter
55 g (¼ cup firmly packed) brown sugar

kugel
3 sheets *matzo*
6 eggs
110 g (½ cup firmly packed) brown sugar
½ teaspoon ground cinnamon
½ teaspoon salt
1 Granny Smith apple, peeled and grated
115 g (1 stick/4 oz) butter, melted

topping
55 g (¼ cup firmly packed) brown sugar
2 teaspoons ground cinnamon
cream or ice cream, to serve

Preheat the oven to 180°C (355°F) conventional. Grease a 2 litre (8 cup) ovenproof baking dish.

To make the roasted apples, combine the apple, apple cider vinegar, butter and brown sugar in a separate baking dish. Roast for 40 minutes or until soft, tossing from time to time. Set aside.

To make the kugel, break the *matzo* into roughly 3 cm (1 in) square pieces, place in a bowl, cover with water for a minute, then drain and squeeze out any excess water.

In a separate large bowl, whisk together the eggs, sugar, cinnamon and salt until well combined. Add the grated apple and the roasted apples, drained *matzo* and melted butter. Stir to combine and pour into the prepared baking dish. To make the topping, combine the brown sugar and cinnamon and sprinkle on top. Bake for 45 minutes or until golden brown. Serve warm or at room temperature with cream or ice cream.

Serves 8

Charoset Ice Cream Parfait

Some of us think *charoset* is the best thing on the *seder* table, so when we first tested this ice cream, we couldn't believe no one had thought of it sooner. Use the leftover egg whites to whip up a batch of the Brown Sugar Meringues (page 212), which are also *Pesach* friendly, or freeze for another time.
— MMCC

1 tablespoon unsalted butter
60 g (¼ cup) brown sugar
1 Granny Smith apple, peeled and chopped
3 medjool dates, pitted and finely chopped
2 dried figs, finely chopped
2 tablespoons sultanas
½ teaspoon ground cinnamon
60 ml (¼ cup) sweet Passover wine or port
750 ml (3 cups) thickened cream
115 g (½ cup) caster sugar
3 egg yolks
⅛ teaspoon salt
50 g (⅓ cup) roasted almonds, chopped, plus extra

Start this recipe the day before. You will need a 1.5 litre (6 cup) lined loaf pan or freezeproof container.

Heat the butter in a small saucepan over medium heat. When the butter has melted and looks foamy, add the brown sugar and mix it in. Add the apple and toss for a minute. Add the date, fig and sultanas and cook, stirring, for about a minute, until the fruit is well coated. Add the cinnamon and wine or port. Bring to the boil, then reduce the heat to low, cover and cook for 10 minutes, stirring from time to time. Remove from the heat and mash the fruit slightly. Set aside.

While the fruit is cooking, heat 500 ml (2 cups) of the cream in a medium saucepan over medium heat until bubbles appear around the edges. Set aside. Using an electric mixer, beat the caster sugar, egg yolks and salt for a few minutes until pale and thick. Gradually add the heated cream and beat together thoroughly. Return the mixture to the saucepan and cook over medium heat, stirring constantly, for 8 minutes or until it forms a thin custard and the mixture coats the back of a spoon (you should be able to lift the spoon from the saucepan and run your finger along the back, leaving a clear trail). Add the fruit mixture and allow to cool.

In a separate bowl, whisk the remaining cream until soft peaks form. Fold the cream into the cooled mixture along with the roasted almonds. Pour into your prepared pan or container, cover with plastic wrap, and refrigerate for at least 2 hours or until cold, then place in the freezer and freeze overnight. Every few hours, if possible (while you are awake!), take the container out of the freezer and give the mixture a good stir.

The mixture can also be churned in an ice-cream machine. Slice or scoop the parfait and top with extra roasted almonds, to serve. Makes about 6 cups.
Serves 8

Almond Lemon Chiffon

You just won't believe it. No dairy, no gluten, *Pesach*-friendly and one of the best, light yet moist, lemony cakes you'll ever make. This recipe will become a year-round staple. Even though it's made the same way as a traditional chiffon, don't expect the same height. But expect the same deliciousness. — MMCC

finely grated zest of 1 lemon
180 g (¾ cup/6⅓ oz) caster sugar
6 eggs, separated
25 ml lemon juice (juice of approx ½ lemon)
1 teaspoon vanilla extract
200 g (1¾ cup/7 oz) ground almonds (almond meal)
1 teaspoon baking powder
⅛ teaspoon salt

lemon icing
240 g (1¾ cups) icing sugar mixture
45 ml (2 tablespoons + 1 teaspoon) lemon juice

Preheat the oven to 180°C (355°F) conventional.

You will need a high-sided angel cake (chiffon) tin that is not non-stick, has a centre funnel and removable base. Do not grease it.

In the bowl of an electric mixer fitted with the paddle attachment, combine lemon zest and half the caster sugar and mix for a minute or so to release the citrus oils. Add the egg yolks to the bowl and beat until pale and creamy. Mix in the lemon juice and vanilla until just combined.

Place the almond meal and baking powder in a small bowl and mix to combine. Using a silicone spatula, fold the almond mixture into the egg yolk mixture.

In a separate bowl, using the electric mixer, whisk the egg whites and salt until soft peaks form. While continuing to whisk, slowly add the remaining caster sugar and whisk until the whites are just stiff and glossy.

Using a spatula, fold one-third of the egg whites into the batter to lighten it, then very gently fold the remainder of the egg whites into the lightened batter until just incorporated.

Pour the mixture into the tin and bake for 30 minutes or until a skewer inserted into the cake comes out clean.

After removing the cake from the oven, immediately invert the tin onto a wire rack. The cake needs to be suspended upside down until it is cool to stop it from collapsing.

When completely cool, turn the tin right-side up and run a knife around the outside of the cake and the funnel, literally cutting the cake away from the sides of the tin. Holding the funnel, lift the base out of the tin. Use the knife to cut between the cake and the base. Invert the cake onto your serving plate and remove the funnel piece.

To make the lemon icing, place the icing sugar mixture in a small bowl. Add half the lemon juice and mix with a spatula until combined, then add the remaining juice, little by little as needed, until very smooth with a thick pouring consistency. You may not need all the lemon juice or you may need just a little more. Spoon the icing on top of the cake, without touching the surface of the cake with your spoon to avoid crumbs, allowing some to drip down the sides.

Serves 8–10

Nut-Free Chocolate Torte

Despite all the nutty deliciousness, there are times when we just need a nut-free *Pesach* cake. So we searched and discussed, and tested and tasted, as many nut-free, flour-free cakes as we could find. This one ticked all the boxes: a simple yet delightfully intense chocolate cake that also happens to be *Pesach*-perfect. This cake might crack, but consider it part of its rustic charm. – MMCC

150 g (5⅓ oz) dark chocolate, roughly chopped
150 g (5⅓ oz) unsalted butter
4 eggs, separated
⅛ teaspoon salt
150 g (⅔ cup) caster sugar
whipped cream, to serve

Preheat the oven to 160°C (320°F) conventional. Line a 20 cm (8 in) springform tin.

Using a double boiler or microwave, melt the chocolate with the butter (see Kitchen Notes, page 13). Stir until just smooth and set aside to cool.

Using an electric mixer, whisk the egg whites and salt until frothy and opaque. While continuing to whisk, slowly add half the sugar and whisk until soft peaks form. Set aside.

In a separate bowl, whisk the yolks with the remaining sugar for 5 minutes or until thick and pale. Add the cooled chocolate mixture and slowly whisk to combine.

Using a spatula, fold a large spoonful of the egg whites into the chocolate mixture, then gently fold in the remainder until just combined.

Pour the mixture into the prepared tin. Bake for 35 minutes or until just set but still a little wobbly.

Serve with whipped cream.

Serves 8

Chocolate Walnut Cake

This is one of my favourite cakes to make during *Pesach*. Actually, I love it so much I make it throughout the year. As a keen baker, I've always found the method of beating egg yolks into the whisked egg whites very unusual, yet very successful. Gluten-free, dairy-free and even better the next day, it is such a winner for me. — NATANYA

100 g (⅓ cup + 1½ tablespoons) caster sugar
finely grated zest of 1 orange
4 eggs, separated
⅛ teaspoon salt
115 g (4 oz) dark chocolate, grated or finely chopped
115 g (4 oz) ground walnuts

chocolate glaze
150 g (5⅓ oz) dark chocolate
1½ tablespoons caster sugar
1½ teaspoons unsalted butter or oil
90 ml (⅓ cup + 2 teaspoons) water

Preheat the oven to 180°C (355°F) conventional. Line a 20 cm (8 in) springform cake tin.

Using a spatula, mix the caster sugar and orange zest in a bowl for a minute or so to release the citrus oils.

Using an electric mixer, whisk the egg whites and salt in a separate bowl until soft peaks form and, while continuing to whisk, slowly add the sugar. Continue to whisk until thick and glossy. Add the egg yolks, one at a time, whisking well after each addition.

Using a spatula, gently fold in the chocolate and the ground walnut. Pour the mixture into the prepared tin and bake for 45 minutes or until a skewer inserted into the middle comes out clean. The cake will dip a little when it comes out of the oven. Cool in the tin.

To make the glaze, place the chocolate, sugar, butter or oil and water in a small saucepan and heat over low heat, stirring from time to time, until it is a smooth and shiny glaze. Set aside to cool until it is a thick, pourable cream consistency.

Pour the glaze over the cake and spread over the edge with a spatula.

Serves 8

TIP: You can use a food processor to finely chop the walnuts (if using whole walnuts), taking care not to over-process into a paste, and to grate or finely chop the chocolate.

Coconut Almond Macaroons

We all grew up with the joy of popping the tin of the Manischewitz Coconut Macaroons at the start of *Pesach* and slowly (well, maybe quickly) eating them. They were soft and surprisingly chewy, and often the most delicious, sweet thing on offer. They have since become a nostalgic, essential flavour of *Pesach*, and we're happy we can now make our own – even better – version. A dip of chocolate on the bottom adds an extra layer of texture and deliciousness. – MMCC

2 egg whites
160 g (2½ cups) shredded coconut
140 g (⅔ cup) caster sugar
65 g (⅔ cup) ground almonds (almond meal)
⅛ teaspoon salt
100 g (3½ oz) dark chocolate

Preheat the oven to 175°C (350°F) conventional. Line a large baking tray.

In a small bowl, whisk the egg whites until just opaque. In a separate medium bowl, mix together the coconut, sugar, ground almond and salt. Add the whisked egg white and mix well. Place a small-walnut-sized mound (approx 15 g/½ oz) of the mixture on the prepared tray and lightly squeeze the mound so that the mixture stays together. It does not need to be smooth or compressed. Repeat with the remaining mixture.

Bake for 15 minutes or until crisp on the outside and a little soft in the centre. Cook a little longer if you prefer them crisp, and a little less for chewy. Allow to cool on a wire rack.

Once cool, melt the chocolate in the microwave or double boiler (see Kitchen Notes, page 13).

You will need a wire rack set on top of a piece of baking paper to catch the drips. Dip the bases of the macaroons in the melted chocolate then place on the cake rack until the chocolate has set.

Store in an airtight container for up to 2 weeks.

Makes about 30

TIP: To make chocolate macaroons, add 1⅓ teaspoons cocoa powder and an additional 80 g (3 oz) melted dark chocolate to the mix.

CHAPTER SEVEN

Shavuot

This is a seriously delicious festival with cheese, cheese and more cheese. Cheesecakes are the first thing we turn to, but it's also the time to make traditional Cheese and Sultana *Blintzes* (page 204) and creamy Potato Gratin (page 203).

There are a number of reasons offered as to why it is a custom to eat dairy on *Shavuot*. We like this one: when Moses received the Ten Commandments on Mount Sinai in the 14th century BCE, it was Sabbath in the desert, and the new rules of keeping kosher meant the meat – which they had already prepared – was not in fact allowed. They had no choice but to eat a dairy meal.

The festival of *Shavuot* falls most often in June, exactly seven weeks (the 49 days of the *omer*) after *Pesach*. It celebrates the giving of the Ten Commandments and the *Torah* (the first five books of the Hebrew bible, aka the Old Testament) to Moses and the Israelites on Mount Sinai. It was at that moment the Israelites became known as the Jewish people.

Some people celebrate by reading the Ten Commandments, staying up all night to study *torah,* and others just by diving into cheesecake.

Baked Cheesecake (page 210) and Ricotta Cheesecake Slice (page 208).

Cheese Borekas

Crisp, golden, sesame-encrusted, cheese-filled triangular pastries … this recipe hits the festival trifecta as it is perfect for *Shavuot* (cheese filling), *Sukkot* (it's stuffed) and *Purim* (*hamantashen* shape). It's a really easy rough puff pastry, perfect for our home kitchens. It also works with margarine for those who want a *pareve* (dairy-free) pastry. Imagine Grand Final meat pies and sausage rolls! – MMCC

pastry
225 g (1½ cups/8 oz) plain flour, plus extra
75 g (½ cup/2⅔ oz) self-raising flour
½ teaspoon salt
1½ tablespoons oil
1½ tablespoons white vinegar
125 ml (½ cup) water
150 g (5⅓ oz) unsalted butter, at room temperature

filling
230 g (8 oz) feta, grated
120 g (4 oz) mozzarella, grated
2 shallots (spring onions), finely sliced
1 egg
1 egg yolk
salt
ground black pepper

to glaze
1 egg white, beaten
2 tablespoons sesame seeds

Start this recipe the day before.

To make the pastry, in the bowl of an electric mixer fitted with the dough hook, combine the flours, salt, oil and vinegar. Gradually add the water and mix until the pastry comes together. Shape the pastry into a disc, wrap in plastic wrap and refrigerate for 2 hours.

Using a rolling pin, on a lightly floured surface, roll out the pastry into a rectangle, about 30 x 21 cm (11¾ x 8¼ in), with the short edge facing you. Divide the butter into 3 equal parts; make sure it is easily spreadable. Using a table knife, spread one part of the butter over the pastry and fold into three, like a letter – fold the top third down to the centre, then the bottom third up and over. Spread half of the next part of the butter on the top and fold it in half crossways. Wrap and refrigerate for 2 hours.

Repeat the process once more, rolling out the pastry into a rectangle and spreading one part of the butter, folding into three, spreading the remaining (half part) butter on top and folding in half again. All the butter should now be spread. Wrap and refrigerate for at least 2 hours or overnight before using.

To make the filling combine the feta, mozzarella, shallot, egg and egg yolk in a medium bowl. Mix well and season to taste. Refrigerate if not using immediately.

Preheat the oven to 180°C (355°F) conventional and line a large baking tray. On a well-floured board, using a floured rolling pin, roll the pastry out to a 50 x 30 cm (20 × 12 in) rectangle. If the butter starts to leak out of the layers, refrigerate to firm up. Cut into 15 squares, around 10 x 10 cm (4 x 4 in) each. Place a tablespoon of the filling in the centre of each. Brush the edges with a little water, fold the square to form a triangle and press to seal. Using the flat side of the knife blade, press down firmly along the two edges to seal completely. Place on the prepared tray.

Brush each boreka with egg white, sprinkle with sesame seeds and bake for 30 minutes or until golden.

Serve warm or at room temperature.
Makes 15

TIP: For cheese and spinach borekas, add 2 handfuls (approx 80 g/3 oz) baby spinach leaves, finely chopped, to the filling.

Salmon
with Tahina and Herbs

If you've eaten at my place you would know how much I love serving a side of salmon. Because it tastes fabulous, because it feeds a crowd, because it looks stunning, and also because I then serve a rich *milchig* (dairy) dessert. The inspiration for this dish comes from the late chef Greg Malouf's Salmon Tarator when it featured in Maeve O'Meara's *Food Safari* book alongside one of our recipes.
— MERELYN

tahina yoghurt sauce
60 g (¼ cup) tahini
250 g (1 cup) plain unsweetened Greek yoghurt
2 tablespoons lemon juice
1 clove garlic, crushed
½ teaspoon salt

salmon
1 small side (about 1 kg/2 lb 3 oz) sustainably sourced salmon, pin boned
juice of ½ lemon
1 tablespoon extra-virgin olive oil
1 teaspoon salt
ground black pepper

herb salad
½ red onion, finely sliced
juice of 1 lemon
1 large handful flat-leaf parsley, leaves only
1 large handful mint, leaves only
50 g (½ cup) walnuts, toasted and roughly chopped
1 long red chilli, seeded and finely sliced
2 tablespoons extra-virgin olive oil
½ teaspoon ground sumac
½ teaspoons salt
¼ teaspoon ground black pepper

to sprinkle
1 teaspoon ground sumac

To make the yoghurt sauce, mix the tahini with the yoghurt, lemon juice, garlic and salt. Stir until it forms a thick sauce. Season to taste with extra lemon juice and salt, as needed. Cover and refrigerate until needed.

To make the salmon, preheat the oven to 200°C (390°F) conventional. Line a large baking tray and place the side of salmon on it. Drizzle with the lemon juice and olive oil then sprinkle with the salt and a little pepper. Place in the oven and cook for 15 minutes for rare or 20 minutes for medium. The salmon will continue to cook as it cools down so allow a few minutes less than you might think. Remove from the oven and allow to cool to room temperature, about 30 minutes.

While the salmon is cooling, make the herb salad. Place the onion in a large bowl and mix with the lemon juice. Set aside for 20 minutes until the onion has softened to a quick pickle. Roughly chop the parsley and mint and place in the bowl with the onion. Add the walnut and chilli. Toss together then add the olive oil, sumac, salt and pepper and toss again. Taste for seasoning and adjust as needed.

Lift the baking paper with the salmon onto a platter. Spread the tahina yoghurt sauce all over the top of the salmon, then top with the herb salad and sprinkle with the sumac to serve.
Serves 8

MMCC Eggplant Parmigiana

This simple, slow-cooked eggplant and tomato bake has been part of my repertoire for years and is a firm favourite in my house. So much so that I always have a few batches of the MMCC Tomato Sauce in the freezer, ready to go. These days I layer it with cheese and basil, which takes it to a new level and makes it an excellent meat-free meal with a fresh green salad on the side. – NATANYA

MMCC Tomato Sauce
1½ tablespoons extra-virgin olive oil
1 onion, finely chopped
1½ tablespoons tomato paste
1 clove garlic, whole
800 g (1 lb 12 oz) tinned diced tomatoes
½ teaspoon salt
⅛ teaspoon ground black pepper

eggplant
2 eggplants
125 ml (½ cup) extra-virgin olive oil
¼ teaspoon salt
ground black pepper
160 g (6 oz) fresh mozzarella or bocconcini
50 g (½ cup) grated parmesan
10 basil leaves, torn

Grease a 1.5 litre (6 cup) ovenproof dish.

Preheat the oven to 180°C (355°F). Line two large baking trays.

To make the tomato sauce, heat the oil over medium-low heat in a deep frying pan or large saucepan with a lid. Add the onion, cover and cook for 5 minutes. Uncover and cook for a further 15 minutes, stirring from time to time, until completely soft and a little translucent but not brown. Add the tomato paste and garlic and cook for a minute or two, stirring from time to time, then add the tomatoes, salt and pepper. Reduce the heat to low and simmer uncovered for 2 hours, stirring from time to time, until a rich sauce forms. Remove the garlic, check the seasoning and set aside.

Meanwhile, slice the eggplant into 1 cm (½ in) slices. Brush both sides of each slice with the olive oil, season with salt and pepper, and place in one layer on the prepared trays. Roast for 30 minutes or until soft and golden on the edges.

Slice the mozzarella or bocconcini and tear the slices into smaller pieces. Spoon a little of the tomato sauce into the prepared dish to cover the base. Layer eggplant, a scant layer of tomato sauce, mozzarella or bocconcini, parmesan and basil into the dish, finishing with a layer of cheese on top.

Bake for 30 minutes until bubbling, golden and well cooked.

Allow to cool slightly before serving.

Serves 6 as a main

TIP: This sauce takes a few hours to cook so it is worthwhile making a bigger batch and freezing some for another day.

Potato Gratin

I was taught to make potato gratin by my adopted French mother while living in France in my twenties, and have been perfecting it ever since. This version is my ultimate. Par-cooking the potatoes in milk and cream with the garlic and herbs infuses a delicate flavour through the dish. It tastes perfect when served freshly made, but I am equally happy reheating it the next day when all the flavours have become best friends and mingle together. — MERELYN

1 tablespoon unsalted butter
1.2 kg (2 lbs 10 oz) (about 6 medium) desiree or other waxy potatoes
310 ml (1¼ cups) milk
160 ml (⅔ cup) pure cream
1 bay leaf
2 teaspoons salt
ground black pepper
1 clove garlic, crushed
2 sprigs thyme, leaves only
pinch of nutmeg
1 teaspoon plain flour, cornflour or potato flour

Preheat the oven to 180°C (355°F). Generously grease a 1.5 litre (6 cup) gratin dish or shallow ovenproof dish with a little of the butter.

Peel and thinly slice the potatoes. Place the milk, cream, remaining butter, bay leaf, 1 teaspoon of the salt and a generous grind of black pepper in a large saucepan and bring to the boil. Reduce the heat to medium-low and simmer for 5 minutes, stirring constantly to stop the milk from catching on the bottom of the pan. Remove the bay leaf.

Add the potato to the pan, return to a simmer and cook for 10 minutes or until just tender, stirring very regularly to stop the mixture sticking to the bottom of the pan and burning. Remove from the heat.

Gently stir in the garlic, thyme and nutmeg until combined. Sift the flour on top and stir through gently.

Layer the potato in the prepared dish, seasoning each layer with the remaining salt and pepper. Pour over any remaining liquid. Bake for 1 hour or until the potatoes are golden brown and soft (pierce with a sharp knife to check). If it gets too dark, cover with foil. Remove from the oven and leave to sit for around 10 minutes before serving.

Serves 6

Cheese and Sultana *Blintzes*

Diving into a warm crepe stuffed with a soft, billowy cream-cheese filling is one of our absolute *Shavuot* highlights. This makes 20 crepes using an 18 cm (7¾ in) pan. Use as many as you need and any remaining filled *blintzes* can be refrigerated for up to 3 days or frozen for up to 1 month. Cook straight from the fridge or freezer, adding a few extra minutes in the oven. — MERELYN

crepe batter
375 ml (1½ cups) milk
2 eggs
75 g (2½ oz) unsalted butter, melted, plus ½ teaspoon extra
2 teaspoons caster sugar
½ teaspoon salt
150 g (1 cup) plain flour

cheese filling
500 g (1 lb 2 oz) cream cheese, at room temperature
125 g (½ cup + 2 teaspoons) caster sugar
2 egg yolks
2½ tablespoons sour cream
finely grated zest of ½ lemon
1 teaspoon vanilla extract
80 g (½ cup) sultanas

to serve
Rhubarb Strawberry Compote (page 215)
sour cream

To make the crepe batter, using a stick blender or food processor, combine the milk, eggs, melted butter, sugar and salt. Add the flour and mix until you have a smooth batter with no lumps. Cover and refrigerate for at least 1 hour and up to 24 hours.

To fry the crepes, heat a small crepe pan or flat non-stick frying pan over medium heat. It works well to transfer the batter into a jug for easy pouring. Add a pea-sized knob of butter to the pan and, when just sizzling, pour in a little batter. Swirl the pan so the batter covers the base and tip out any excess back into the jug. You don't want the crepe to be too thin or too thick. Cook gently over medium heat for a couple of minutes until you can gently lift an edge and peek underneath. When the underside is lightly browned all over, slide the crepe onto a large plate, uncooked side up. You will only be cooking one side of the crepe. You will most likely not need to grease the pan after the first crepe. Continue with the rest of the batter, piling the crepes on top of each other. Allow to cool before filling.

To make the filling, in a medium bowl, beat the cream cheese and sugar with an electric mixer until light and smooth. Add the egg yolks and beat. Add the sour cream, lemon zest and vanilla and beat to combine. Stir through the sultanas.

Butter a baking dish big enough so the blintzes can fit in one layer.

To fill the crepe, lay one crepe flat on a clean surface, uncooked side up. Place 2 tablespoons of the filling in the centre of the crepe, and shape into a log around 7 x 2 cm (3 x 1 in). Fold the left and right sides of the crepe over towards the middle and roll up from the edge closest to you until you have a small rectangular *blintz* (or parcel). Place the *blintz*, seam-side down, in the prepared dish. Continue until all the crepes are filled.

To finish cooking the *blintzes*, preheat the oven to 180°C (355°F) conventional.

Cover the baking dish with foil and cook for 20 minutes until the blintzes are slightly puffed and the filling is hot.

Alternatively, you can finish cooking them in a well-buttered frying pan over medium-low heat for a few minutes on each side until golden all over and cooked through.

Serve warm with Rhubarb Strawberry Compote and sour cream.

Makes around 20 blintzes

Sweet Cheese *Lokshen* Kugel

This nostalgic sweet noodle pudding originated from my beautiful grandmother, Sarah, and I treasure the original faded recipe she wrote out by hand. I grew up with my mother often making it for my brothers and me as the ultimate comfort food. I remember always going back for more, fishing out as many sultanas as I could find! I have taken those wonderful memories and made the recipe even richer and more comforting for the generations that follow me. The legacy continues.
— NATANYA

100 g (3½ oz) *lokshen* or dried egg fettucine
1 tablespoon unsalted butter
150 g (5⅓ oz) ricotta
150 g (5⅓ oz) cream cheese, at room temperature
1½ tablespoons caster sugar
¼ teaspoon salt
1 teaspoon vanilla extract
1 egg
1 Granny Smith apple, peeled and grated
45 g (¼ cup) sultanas
60 ml (¼ cup) pure cream
2 tablespoons cinnamon sugar (see Kitchen Notes, page 13), to sprinkle

Grease a 1.5 litre (6 cup), about 20 x 25 cm (8 x 10 in), baking dish.
Preheat the oven to 180°C (355°F) conventional.
Bring a large saucepan of water to the boil. Add the *lokshen*, reduce heat to medium and cook, according to the packet instructions, until al dente. Drain, return to the pot, mix in the butter and set aside.
Using an electric mixer, beat the ricotta and cream cheese with the sugar, salt and vanilla until smooth. Add the egg and beat until combined then add the apple and sultanas and gently beat to combine. Using a spatula, fold in the cream and the *lokshen* and pour into the prepared dish. Top with the cinnamon sugar.
Bake for 35 minutes or until just set and golden around the edges.
Serve warm or at room temperature (or straight from the fridge the next day).
Serves 6

Ricotta Cheesecake Slice

As a teenager, before I understood the importance of collecting recipes properly, I was obsessed with my Auntie Leah's cheesecake. It was dense but also light, not too sweet and had a pastry lattice on the top. I have never been able to replicate it. I have tried various iterations of various cheesecakes, always with hers in mind. I have ended up with this: a glorious ricotta cheesecake slice that reminds me of the old world. — LISA

pastry
240 g (1⅓ cups/7 oz) self-raising flour, plus extra
85 g (3 oz) cold unsalted butter, chopped
55 g (¼ cup/1¾ oz) caster sugar
⅛ teaspoon salt
1 egg yolk
50 g (1¾ oz) sour cream

filling
400 g (14 oz) ricotta (drained, if wet) or quark (European cottage cheese)
115 g (½ cup/3½ oz) caster sugar
4 eggs, separated
150 g (5⅓ oz) sour cream
½ teaspoon vanilla extract
finely grated zest of 1 lemon
1 tablespoon plain flour
pinch of salt

Preheat the oven to 170°C (340°F) conventional.

Line the base and butter the sides of a rectangular slice tin or shallow baking dish, approx 32 x 23 x 3 cm (12 x 9 x 1¼ in).

To make the pastry, combine the flour, butter, sugar and salt in a food processor and pulse until it forms crumbs. In a small bowl, mix the egg yolk and sour cream then add to the processor. Pulse until a ball is formed around the blade. Divide the pastry in two, for the base and for the lattice.

To make the lattice, flour a piece of baking paper larger than the tin. With a floured rolling pin, roll out one piece of the pastry evenly on the paper until it is around 2–3 mm (1/10 in) thick. Trim off the rough edges, then cut into 2.5 cm (1 in) wide strips. Do not move the strips. Gather the scraps and repeat on another piece of paper. You are aiming for four strips that can be trimmed to 32 cm (12½ in) and four strips trimmed to 23 cm (9 in) in length. Place the paper(s) and pastry strips onto a tray and refrigerate.

To make the base, on a lightly floured piece of baking paper slightly bigger than the tin, roll the other piece of pastry into a tin-sized rectangle. Flip the paper over onto the tin, so the pastry is facing downwards, remove the paper and gently press into the base so it is completely covered. Patch any cracks. Bake for 10 minutes then remove from the oven and set aside.

To make the filling, using an electric mixer, beat the ricotta or quark with the sugar until smooth. Add the yolks, sour cream, vanilla and lemon zest and beat well. Add the flour and beat to combine. In a separate bowl, whisk the egg whites with a pinch of salt until soft peaks form. Gently fold the egg whites into the ricotta mixture and pour into the pastry-lined tin.

Take the lattice from the fridge. Gently arrange the strips, the shorter ones across the shorter direction and the longer ones across the longer, on the top of the filling. Trim any overhang.

Place in the oven and bake for 45 minutes or until puffed and golden on top and with just a slight wobble.

Remove from the oven and cool completely before cutting into squares.

Serve at room temperature on the day of baking or store in the fridge and serve chilled.

Serves 12

Baked Cheesecake

This type of biscuit-base, baked cream-cheese cheesecake is a staple in Sydney's Jewish community at *Shavuot*, introduced by the many wonderful cooks from South Africa who now call Australia home. The original version of this super creamy, light and irresistible cheesecake came to us from MMCC founding co-author Lauren Fink. Since then, it has reappeared in *Now for Something Sweet* (2020) and has become an MMCC essential. – MMCC

120 g (4 oz) digestive biscuits
60 g (2¼ oz) unsalted butter, melted
3 eggs, separated
115 g (½ cup/4 oz) caster sugar
375 g (13¼ oz) cream cheese, at room temperature
100 ml (⅓ cup plus 1 tablespoon) pure cream
pinch of salt

Preheat the oven to 160°C (320°F) conventional. Line the base of a 20 cm (8 in) springform tin. Do not grease or line the side.

Process the biscuits in a food processor until a fine crumb forms. Add the melted butter and pulse to combine. Press the mixture evenly into the bottom of the prepared tin. Cook in the oven for 10 minutes. Remove from the oven and leave to cool.

Using an electric mixer, beat the egg yolks with half the sugar on medium speed until pale and light. Add the cream cheese, one-third at a time, and beat on high speed until there are no lumps. Reduce speed to low and slowly add the cream, beating to combine. Set aside.

In a separate bowl, whisk the egg whites and salt on medium speed until soft peaks form. Gradually add the remaining sugar while continuing to whisk until the egg whites are stiff but not dry. Using a spatula, gently fold the egg whites into the cream cheese mixture, one-third at a time.

Pour the mixture on top of the cooked biscuit crust. Place in the oven and bake for 50 minutes or until golden and slightly wobbly.

Turn the oven off, open the oven door slightly and leave to cool completely before removing. The cake will shrink a little and crack. To remove from the tin, gently run a knife around the outside edge of the cake, then unclip.

Serve at room temperature on the day of baking or refrigerate and serve cold.

Serves 8

Brown Sugar Meringues
with Rhubarb Strawberry Compote and Yoghurt Cream

Pretty much every Australian cookbook has a pavlova recipe. For a change we've gone with a 'deconstructed pav', reworking our classic '23-minute' meringues into a perfect dairy dessert, combining them with tart, yet sweet, red rhubarb compote and a rich, tangy yoghurt cream. – MMCC

3 egg whites
⅛ teaspoon salt
125 g (½ cup + 2 teaspoons/ 4½ oz) caster sugar
50 g (¼ cup, firmly packed/2 oz) brown sugar
½ heaped teaspoon cornflour
½ teaspoon white vinegar
½ teaspoon vanilla extract
Rhubarb Strawberry Compote (page 215)
Yoghurt Cream (page 215)

Preheat the oven to 150°C (300°F) conventional. Line a large baking tray.

Using an electric mixer on medium speed, whisk the egg whites with the salt for 8 minutes.

While continuing to whisk, add the caster sugar in a slow stream and whisk for another 8 minutes. Add the brown sugar, cornflour, vinegar and vanilla and continue to whisk for a further 7 minutes. The mixture will be very thick and glossy.

Using a dessert spoon, place 2 spoonfuls of the mixture on top of each other to make a mound on the prepared tray. Repeat with all the mixture, leaving space between each mound. You should have 10 mounds. Place in the middle of the oven and cook for 70 minutes or until firm to the touch. Remove from the oven and allow to cool on the tray. Store in an airtight container for up to 3 days.

Makes 10 meringues

TIP: While we have combined three recipes (the meringue, cream and compote, on page 215) to make a stunning dessert, they can also be served individually, paired with your favourite sweet treat.

Rhubarb Strawberry Compote

1 bunch rhubarb, trimmed (about 500 g/1 lb 2 oz once trimmed)
90 g (½ cup, lightly packed) brown sugar
1 teaspoon vanilla extract
2 strips orange peel
250 g (9 oz) strawberries, hulled and thinly sliced

Preheat the oven to 200°C (390°F) conventional.

Slice the rhubarb into 1 cm (½ in) pieces and place in a small roasting pan. Add the sugar, vanilla and orange peel and toss. Roast, uncovered, for 15 minutes or until the rhubarb is starting to break down and it bubbles around the edges. Stir in the strawberries and cook for another 5 minutes. Remove from the oven, stir again and leave to cool.

Makes about 2½ cups

Yoghurt Cream

250 ml (1 cup) pure cream
1 tablespoon caster sugar
125 g (½ cup) unsweetened plain Greek yoghurt

Whisk the cream and sugar together until soft peaks form. Using a spatula, fold through the Greek yoghurt. Refrigerate until ready to assemble or serve.

To serve, either layer and pile up the meringues, compote and cream on a platter, like an Eton Mess, or serve each item separately at the table for people to help themselves.

Serves 6–8

CHAPTER EIGHT

Shiva + Comfort

Following the death of an immediate family member, there is a traditional mourning period of seven days, known as *Shiva*, when those who are grieving focus on their loss and are meant to do as little as possible. It is a time when the community provides a cocoon of warmth and support. Friends and peers, old and new, extended family and others, drop by with words of comfort, unique insights and, often, a plate of food.

For those in mourning, the first meal after the funeral (*seudat havra'ah*) traditionally includes hard-boiled eggs, the symbol of life and hope, or bagels to represent the circle of life.

When Merelyn lost her dear mum Yoland, Lisa arrived at the door with a 'Tupperware' filled to the brim with vanilla-scented, buttery Almond *Kifli* (page 238), an iconic Austro-Hungarian biscuit Merelyn's mother used to make. It warmed her heart to taste flavours of her childhood and reminisce about those precious times spent baking with her mum.

Over the years, we've been to many houses of *Shiva* and seen tables laden with comfort food. And not just any comfort food. We have a theory that people bring their most-loved dishes to shower love on a grieving family. We have often joked, and, yes, we see it's not that funny, that we should have used *Shiva* houses to find recipes for our MMCC project.

The dishes in this chapter go beyond the seven days of *Shiva*. Food is our band-aid in challenging times. A baby born, a new house, someone sick, someone in need. These are recipes of love, support and sustenance, which are easily made, packed and carried. Arriving with a plate, a box, a tub, is just what we do.

Chicken Barley Soup (page 220).

Roasted Carrot and Cauli Soup

I make this recipe all winter long for my family. It is also my go-to for sharing when someone is in need of extra care. I call it my winter soup as it is so warming and feels so nourishing. It gets bonus points for being quick and easy to make. The pangrattato, though not essential, takes it to the next level. — NATANYA

1 cauliflower, trimmed and sliced
4 carrots, peeled and sliced
60 ml (¼ cup) olive oil
1 teaspoon salt
¼ teaspoon ground black pepper
1 leek, chopped
¼ teaspoon cayenne pepper
1.5 litres (6 cups) vegetable or chicken stock

pangrattato
125 g (4½ oz) sourdough bread with crust removed
10 sprigs thyme, leaves only
½ teaspoon flaky salt
1 tablespoon extra-virgin olive oil
1 tablespoon melted butter or olive oil
1 teaspoon dried chilli flakes
zest of ½ lemon

Preheat the oven to 200°C (390°F) conventional.

Toss the cauliflower and carrot with half the oil and sprinkle with the salt and black pepper. Spread evenly on a baking tray and roast for 30 minutes, or until golden and tender.

Heat the remaining oil in a large saucepan over medium heat. Add the leek and sauté for 10 minutes, covered, or until softened. Add the cayenne and stir for a minute. Add the roasted vegetables and the stock and simmer for 20 minutes.

In the meantime, to make the pangrattato, reduce the oven temperature to 180°C (355°F) conventional. Place the bread in a food processor with the thyme leaves and salt, and process until roughly chopped. Add the oil, butter (or extra oil if you prefer), chilli and lemon zest then pulse until well combined. Place on a baking tray and bake for 10 minutes or until golden brown.

When the soup is cooked, allow to cool slightly, then puree in a blender or using a stick blender until very smooth. Season to taste with extra salt and pepper, as needed.

Serve bowls of the soup with the pangrattato sprinkled on top. *Serves 6*

Chicken Barley Soup

Dropping this pot of friendship, care and love on someone's doorstep is sometimes all you can do. Start with a rich, flavoursome stock made from a whole chicken. Add more goodness with vegetables, herbs and barley – our favourite grain from the old world – and throw in shredded, succulent chicken to make a heartwarming, soul-soothing meal in a bowl. – MMCC

chicken stock and chicken

1 x 1.4 kg (3 lb 1 oz/size 14) chicken, quartered
3 litres (12 cups) water
1 carrot, quartered
1 parsnip, quartered
1 onion, quartered
2 celery sticks, with leaves, roughly chopped
1 handful flat-leaf parsley
1 tablespoon black peppercorns
1 tablespoon salt

barley soup

60 ml (¼ cup) extra-virgin olive oil
2 leeks, chopped
2 carrots, roughly chopped
2 celery sticks, chopped
½ teaspoon salt
¼ teaspoon ground black pepper
1 clove garlic, bruised
4 roma tomatoes, peeled and roughly chopped
1 bay leaf
8 sprigs thyme, leaves only
1.5 litres (6 cups) reserved chicken stock
200 g (1 scant cup/7 oz) pearl barley
¼ cup flat-leaf parsley leaves, chopped

To make the stock and cook the chicken, place the chicken and water in a stockpot. Bring to the boil and skim off the scum that rises to the top. Add the remaining ingredients and bring to the boil. Reduce the heat to medium-low and simmer for 1 hour, partially covered. Carefully lift the chicken out of the stockpot, remove the breast meat and wings and set aside. (Careful, it's hot, rubber gloves may help.)

Return the remaining chicken and bones to the stock and simmer for another hour. Allow the stock to cool a little, then remove the chicken and take all the remaining meat off the bones. Set aside the meat and discard the bones. Strain the stock, set aside and discard the stock vegetables.

To make the barley soup, using the same stockpot (which may need a rinse), heat the oil over medium heat and sauté the leek, carrot, celery, salt and pepper for 20 minutes or until soft. Add the garlic, tomato, bay leaf, thyme and reserved stock and bring to the boil. Add the barley and reduce the heat to a simmer. Cook, covered, for 45 minutes or until the barley is tender. Remove and discard the garlic clove. Break up the chicken meat and add to the soup, along with the parsley. Stir through to heat. Season to taste with extra salt and pepper.

Serves 6–8

Glazed Chicken Meatloaf

There's meatloaf, and then there's this meatloaf. Lisa first fell in love with 'Raie's Meatloaf' at Raie's Deli, in the late 1970s. Natty and Merelyn can still recall the excitement when they tasted the original recipe (with beef mince) for our first book. Deliciously glazed and sauced, this succulent chicken loaf is easy to bake, cool, wrap up and deliver to a friend or family in need. – MMCC

1 kg (2 lb 3 oz) chicken mince
1 onion, grated
1 carrot, peeled and grated
1 egg, beaten
70 g (1 cup) fresh breadcrumbs
2 cloves garlic, crushed
1 tablespoon tomato paste
2 tablespoons worcestershire sauce
1 handful flat-leaf parsley, leaves chopped
1 teaspoon salt
½ teaspoon ground black pepper

glaze
125 ml (½ cup) tomato passata
125 ml (½ cup) worcestershire sauce
90 g (½ cup, lightly packed) brown sugar
160 ml (⅔ cup) water

Preheat the oven to 180°C (355°F) conventional. Lightly grease a large baking dish.

To make the glaze, in a small bowl mix together the tomato passata, worcestershire sauce, brown sugar and water until well combined and the sugar is dissolved. Set aside.

In a large bowl, mix together the chicken mince, onion, carrot, egg, breadcrumbs, garlic, tomato paste, worcestershire sauce, parsley, salt and pepper until well combined. Place the meat mixture into the baking dish. With wet hands, shape the mixture into a long log. The thinner and longer the log the more (delicious) crust there will be. If you prefer, make two smaller logs, one for you, one to gift.

Pour the glaze mixture over the meatloaf and place in the oven. Roast for 1 hour, basting often, until glazed and brown.

Serves 6

TIP: To make fresh breadcrumbs, remove the crusts from good-quality white bread or sourdough and process until fine crumbs are formed.

Rice and Beef Paprikash

Substantial and satisfying, rice paprikash is a one-pot meal that warms the soul and fills the tummy with a generous mixture of beef (or veal) paprikash and risotto-like rice. As a little girl I thought this recipe was my mother's creation, but, when I moved to Sydney, I quickly learnt it is a Hungarian staple. It is slow-cooked goodness, easy to transport and possibly even better reheated. — MERELYN

60 ml (¼ cup) extra-virgin olive oil
500 g (1 lb 2 oz) diced gravy beef or veal
2 onions, chopped
2 heaped teaspoons sweet Hungarian paprika
⅛ teaspoon cayenne pepper, or to taste
2 cloves garlic, crushed
½ red capsicum, chopped
1 carrot, chopped
2 tomatoes, finely chopped
125 ml (½ cup) white wine
250 ml (1 cup) chicken stock
165 g (¾ cup) long-grain rice
1 teaspoon salt
¼ teaspoon ground black pepper

You will need a flameproof casserole dish or deep frying pan with a lid.

Heat the oil in the pan over medium heat. Working in batches, sauté the beef or veal until well browned. Set aside. Add the onion to the pan and fry for 20 minutes or until dark golden. Add the paprika, cayenne and garlic and cook for a minute until fragrant. Turn the heat to high, add the capsicum, carrot and tomato and toss to combine. Stir in the wine, scraping the bottom of the pan well. Bring to the boil and simmer until evaporated.

Return the meat to the pan and add the stock. Bring to the boil, turn the heat to low and simmer, covered, for 1 hour. If using veal, cook for only 30 minutes.

Add the rice, salt and pepper. Stir to coat. Reduce the heat to low and simmer, covered, for 30 minutes or until the meat is fork tender and the rice is cooked. Fluff with a fork and season to taste.

Serves 4

TIP: For the most authentic flavour, use Kalocsai Hungarian sweet paprika, if you can find it.

Hungarian Beef Goulash

When I was a young girl, my mother made beef goulash, chicken paprikash and schnitzel pretty much every week. She even converted her goulash recipe to the pressure cooker so we were only ever half an hour away from a hearty, warming meal. *Nokedli* and cucumber salad were the standard side dishes; I really had no idea how lucky we were. I silently thank my mother every day. It was such a gift to be tied to the apron strings of an outstanding cook and baker, and now I channel her energy and techniques in my own kitchen. — MERELYN

60 ml (¼ cup) oil
1 kg (2 lb 3 oz) gravy (stewing) beef, cubed
3 onions, chopped
1 heaped tablespoon Hungarian sweet paprika
½ green capsicum, chopped
1 tomato, peeled and chopped
1 teaspoon salt, or to taste
2 teaspoons cornflour, to thicken
80 ml (⅓ cup) water

to serve
Nokedli (page 228)
Cucumber Salad (page 229)

You will need a deep frying pan with a lid or a flameproof casserole dish.

Heat 1 tablespoon of the oil in a deep frying pan over high heat. Working in batches, sear the beef until it is well browned. Remove from the pan and set aside.

Add the remaining oil, reduce the heat to medium and sauté the onion for about 20 minutes or until deep golden. Add the paprika and stir for a minute or until fragrant. Return the beef to the pan and toss with the onion mixture.

Add the capsicum, tomato and salt and toss through. Bring to a simmer, reduce the heat to low and cover with a lid. Cook for 1 hour 30 minutes or until soft and fork tender, adding a little water if it starts to dry out or catch on the bottom of the pan.

In a small bowl, mix the cornflour with the water to make a slurry. Add to the goulash, stirring until slightly thickened. Serve with *Nokedli* and Cucumber Salad (with dill).

Serves 4–6

TIP: For the most authentic flavour, use Kalocsai Hungarian sweet paprika if you can find it.

Nokedli

Deceptively easy to make, *nokedli* are soft, pasta-like Hungarian drop dumplings, similar to German *spaetzle*. The nooks and crannies in their rough shape are perfect for holding the sauce of a paprikash or goulash, or they can be served simply tossed with butter as a side dish. As a young girl I was allowed to 'cut' the *nokedli* dough off a palette knife into the boiling salted water, but it's much easier with a *spaetzle* maker. — **MERELYN**

330 g (2 cups + 2 heaped tablespoons) plain flour
1½ teaspoons salt
2 eggs
250 ml (1 cup) water
2 teaspoons olive oil or butter, to serve

Place the flour and salt in a bowl and make a well in the centre. Add the eggs to the well and beat with a fork. Slowly incorporate the flour, adding a little water at a time until you have a thick batter, about the consistency of porridge. Use a whisk or wooden spoon to beat well until it is smooth. Add a little water if it is too thick.

Bring a large saucepan of salted water to the boil. Using a *spaetzle* maker or a colander and working in batches, push the batter through the holes, letting small pieces fall into the water to cook. The *nokedli* will rise to the surface after a couple of minutes. Continue to boil for a further minute or two or until you taste they are cooked. Remove the *nokedli* with a slotted spoon into a bowl and continue until all the batter is used. Add a little olive oil or butter to the bowl and toss to serve. Reheats well.

Serves 4–6

SEE IMAGE *page 227.*

Cucumber Salad

We've all grown up eating a version of this simple goes-with-absolutely-everything salad, either at home or at one of the many Eastern European restaurants in Sydney. We are so grateful that MMCC founding co-author Jacqui Israel shared her family recipe. – MMCC

125 ml (½ cup) white vinegar
2 teaspoons sugar
1 teaspoon salt
3 large Lebanese cucumbers, sliced
¼ bunch dill, finely chopped, or
    ½ bunch chives, chopped

To make the dressing, mix together the vinegar, sugar and salt in a large container until the sugar and salt is dissolved. Add the cucumber and toss well. Add the dill or chives and refrigerate, covered, for several hours or overnight, tossing again from time to time.

Tip off the excess liquid just before serving.

Serves 6 as a side

TIP: This versatile salad can be matched with many dishes depending on the herbs you use. Chives are lovely with Asian-style dishes (Chicken Sambal, page 34) while dill is a natural fit with European dishes (Beef Goulash, page 226). Aussie barbecue? You can even leave it plain!

SEE IMAGE *page 227.*

Chocolate Sour Cream Kugelhopf

I've been making the original version of this now-updated sour cream bundt cake for decades. It is such a crowd pleaser of a cake and I love the surprise when you cut a slice to reveal the hidden pattern of chocolate and vanilla swirls inside. — NATANYA

to prepare tin
1 tablespoon softened butter
1 tablespoon plain flour

cake
75 g (2⅔ oz) dark chocolate, chopped
1 teaspoon unsweetened cocoa powder
3 eggs
305 g (1⅓ cups/10½ oz) caster sugar
1 teaspoon vanilla extract
200 g (7 oz) unsalted butter, melted
120 g (½ cup/4½ oz) sour cream
250 g (1⅔ cup/9 oz) self-raising flour
½ teaspoon bicarb soda
¼ teaspoon salt
60 ml (¼ cup/2 fl oz) milk
icing sugar, to serve

Preheat the oven to 170°C (340°F) conventional. You will need an 8 cup (21 cm/8½ in) bundt or kugelhopf tin.

To prepare the tin, butter it carefully in every crevice. Tip in the plain flour and shake it from side to side to coat well. Tip out any excess at the sink by turning the tin upside-down and tapping it on the edge. Place in the freezer while you prepare the cake.

In a medium heatproof bowl, melt the chocolate (see Kitchen Notes, page 13). Stir in the cocoa and set aside.

Using an electric mixer on medium speed, beat the eggs, sugar and vanilla until pale and thick. Slowly add the melted butter and sour cream, beating until incorporated.

Sift together the self-raising flour, bicarb soda and salt. With the beater on low speed, add the flour mixture, alternating with the milk, until just incorporated and smooth. Place one-third of the batter (about 300 g/10½ oz) into the bowl with the chocolate mixture and, using a spatula, fold until you have a smooth batter.

Remove the prepared cake tin from the freezer. Drop alternate spoonfuls of the plain and chocolate batters into the tin and pull a skewer or knife backwards and forwards to create the marbling. Be careful to not over-swirl so it does not all mix together.

Bake for 45 minutes or until a skewer inserted comes out clean. Let the cake cool for 10 minutes then turn out onto a wire rack to cool completely. Dust with icing sugar to serve.
Serves 8

TIP: This cake is also beautiful with a Chocolate Glaze (page 190).

Ginger Date Slice

For those of you who love ginger, this is the slice. Warmly spiced and quick to make, this much-loved recipe featured in our first book. Since then, it has become my first sweet choice for a friend in need or for some sweetness at home. I've really amped up the ginger (the more the better for me!) and spice but, if you want to take it down a notch, just leave out the crystallised ginger. — NATANYA

125 g (4½ oz) unsalted butter

200 g (1 cup + 1 tablespoon, lightly packed/3½ oz) brown sugar

150 g (1 cup/5⅓ oz) self-raising flour

½ teaspoon ground ginger

½ teaspoon ground cinnamon

⅛ teaspoon salt

1 egg, lightly beaten

250 g (1½ cups) chopped dried dates

75 g (2⅔ oz) crystallised ginger, chopped

Preheat the oven to 180°C (355°F) conventional. Line a square 20 cm (8 in) baking tin, leaving some of the paper overhanging to help you easily lift the slice out of the tin after baking.

Combine the butter and sugar in a saucepan over a medium-high heat and cook for a few minutes, stirring, until dissolved and melted. Remove from the heat and pour the mixture into a large bowl. Leave to cool slightly.

Sift together the flour, ground ginger, cinnamon and salt. Set aside.

When the butter mixture is cool, add the egg and stir well with a spatula. Fold in the flour mixture, then the dates and crystallised ginger until combined.

Pour into the prepared tin and bake for 35 minutes or until just firm to the touch. Cool in the tin, then lift out using the overhanging paper. Slice into squares to serve. Store in an airtight container for up to 1 week.

Makes about 16 squares

Sour Cherry Chocolate Brownies

After the evening *minyan* service (memorial prayers held during the week of *Shiva*), it is customary for friends and extended family to lay out the food that people have brought over. Everyone mills around, quietly chatting and surrounding the bereaved with love. This amazing brownie is exactly what's needed. Sweet, comforting and the most fudgy brownie I've come across, but, of course, me being me, I had to play with the recipe and add sour cherries. — **NATANYA**

115 g (4 oz) extra-dark chocolate (90%)
225 g (8 oz) dark chocolate (70%)
225 g (8 oz/2 sticks) unsalted butter
460 g (2 cups/1 lb) caster sugar
4 eggs
1 teaspoon vanilla extract
½ teaspoon salt
75 g (½ cup/2¾ oz) plain flour
200 g (1 cup) dried sour red cherries or dried cranberries

Preheat the oven to 160°C (320°F) conventional.

Line a rectangular baking or slice tin (approx 32 x 23 x 3 cm/ 12 x 9 x 1¼ in), leaving some of the paper overhanging to help you easily lift the brownie out of the tin after baking.

Break the chocolate into pieces. Melt the chocolate and butter in a double boiler over simmering water (see Kitchen Notes, page 13) then pour the melted mixture into a large bowl. Add the sugar and, using an electric mixer, beat until smooth. Add the eggs, vanilla and salt and beat well. Using a spatula, gently fold in the flour until just combined then fold in the dried sour cherries or cranberries.

Pour the batter into the prepared tin and smooth the top with a spatula.

Bake for 40 minutes or until the sides begin to pull away from the tin. Allow to cool in the tin. Lift out using the overhanging paper, then cut into squares.

Serves 12

TIP: Add a handful of walnuts for a different texture.

Caraway Kakas and Date Ginger Babas

The first time we came across these Sephardi biscuits was at a *minyan* (prayers during the *Shiva* week) in Sydney. A kind friend had brought bags of freshly baked kakas (savoury caraway ring biscuits) and babas (just-sweet flat date biscuits) to feed the mourners and their visitors. Yet again we were enticed into the delicious, aromatic world of Sephardi cooking and we just had to document the recipe.
— MMCC

biscuit dough
150 g (1 cup/5⅓ oz) plain flour, plus extra
75 g (½ cup/2⅔ oz) self-raising flour
1 tablespoon caster sugar
½ teaspoon salt
100 g (3½ oz) cold unsalted butter
60 ml (¼ cup) chilled water
1 tablespoon oil
½ teaspoon vanilla extract
1 egg, beaten, to glaze

for the kakas
½ teaspoon caraway seeds

for the babas
125 g (4½ oz) medjool dates, pitted and chopped
1 tablespoon butter
125 ml (½ cup) water
1½ tablespoons brown sugar
½ teaspoon ground ginger
2 tablespoons sesame seeds, to sprinkle

Preheat the oven to 200°C (390°F) conventional. Line 2 baking trays.

To make the dough, combine the flours, sugar and salt in a food processor. Pulse to combine. Add the butter and pulse until the mixture resembles breadcrumbs.

In a small bowl, combine the water, oil and vanilla. Add to the flour mixture and pulse until a dough forms around the blade. Divide the dough in half and wrap each piece in plastic wrap. Refrigerate for 1 hour.

To make the kakas, take out one piece of the dough from the refrigerator. Add the caraway seeds and knead a couple of times to evenly distribute. Divide the dough into small walnut-sized balls. With your hands, roll each ball into a thin strand and form a ring, sealing the ends together.

Place on the prepared tray. Brush with the beaten egg to glaze and bake for 15 minutes or until lightly golden. Allow to cool on a wire rack.
Makes 30

To make the filling for the babas, combine the dates, butter and half the water in a small saucepan over medium-low heat. Cook, stirring, for about 10 minutes until the dates have softened. Add the sugar, ginger and remaining water and continue to cook for 10 minutes until the mixture is jam-like and smooth. Allow to cool completely before using.

Take out one piece of the dough from the refrigerator. Lightly flour your benchtop and rolling pin and roll out the dough until it is 3 mm (¹⁄₁₀ in) thick. Using a 5 cm (2 in) cookie cutter, cut out circles. Place about ½ teaspoon of the cooled date jam into the middle of one circle and top with another circle. Press the outside edges to seal. Place on the prepared tray and pat down lightly to flatten a little. Repeat with the remaining dough and date jam.

Brush with the beaten egg to glaze, sprinkle with the sesame seeds and prick the tops several times with a fork. Place on the prepared tray and bake for 15 minutes or until lightly golden. Allow to cool on a wire rack.

Store in an airtight container for up to 2 weeks.
Makes 20

Almond *Kifli*

There are times when a bite of a buttery, melt-in-your-mouth, crumbly vanilla-scented biscuit soothes the soul and, for a moment, makes the world a better place. Almond *kifli* is one of our most treasured heirloom recipes, starting in an Eastern European kitchen many decades ago to then be passed down through the generations to end up here, in Sydney, Australia. – MMCC

65 g (scant ½ cup/2⅓ oz) whole raw almonds (skin on)
125 g (4½ oz) unsalted butter, chopped, at room temperature
175 g (1 cup + 2 tablespoons/ 6¼ oz) plain flour
2 teaspoons caster sugar
½ teaspoon vanilla paste

to finish
65 g (½ cup) vanilla icing sugar (see TIP)

Preheat the oven to 160°C (320°F) conventional. Line a baking tray.

In a food processor, process the almonds until coarsely ground, taking care not to over process and make a paste. Add the butter, flour, caster sugar and vanilla paste. Pulse until a rough dough is formed, taking care not to overwork it. Scrape the bowl down and pulse again until the dough comes together. Take a small ball of dough (if you want to be precise, 12 g/scant ½ oz each) and roll into a thumb-sized log. Bend it slightly into a crescent shape and place on the prepared tray. Repeat with the remaining dough.

Bake for 30 minutes. The biscuit should not brown on top but if you gently lift one up and peek underneath, it should be pale golden. When cool, gently roll the biscuits in the vanilla icing sugar. Store in an airtight container with any excess vanilla icing sugar tipped on top.
Makes 30 biscuits

TIP: To make vanilla icing sugar, halve a vanilla bean lengthwise and scrape the seeds into a container with 500 g (1 lb 2 oz) icing sugar mixture. Roughly chop the vanilla bean and add to the icing sugar. Shake vigorously until the seeds are dispersed, using a whisk to help if needed. Seal the container until ready to use. Lasts for months and months.

Recipe Acknowledgements

We are so grateful to the wonderful cooks who have shared their treasured recipes with us for inclusion in our four books, and now in our fifth. Their original recipes and stories can be seen in our earlier books.

MMCC: Monday Morning Cooking Club (2011)   TFGO: The Feast Goes On (2014)
AATF: Always About the Food (2017)   NFSS: Now for Something Sweet (2020)

Recipe Name	Page	Previous Recipe Name	Book	Cook
Almond Kifli	238	Almond Kifli	MMCC	Sharon Katz
Ashkenazi Cholent	42	Cholent	TFGO	Yvonne Fink
Baked Cheesecake	210	South African Cheescake	NFSS	Dorryce Rock
Baked Cheesecake	210	South African Cheescake	MMCC	Lauren Fink (MMCC)
Boiled Bagels	52	Bagels	TFGO	Shereen Aaron
Braised Red Cabbage	94	Red Cabbage	MMCC	Daphne Doctor
Brown Sugar Meringues	212	23 Minute Meringues	NFSS	Helen Carp
Caraway Kakas and Date Ginger Babas	236	Kakas and Babas	AATF	Rachel Dingoor
Cauliflower and Sweet Potato Pilaf	128	Bengali Rice with Cauliflower	AATF	Tami Weiser
Challah	18	Challah from Heaven	MMCC	Rebbetzin Chanie Wolff
Chargrilled Maple Soy Salmon	83	Maple and Soy Ocean Trout	TFGO	Amber Schwarz
Charoset Ice Cream Parfait	185	Charoset Ice Cream	NFSS	Ronnie Fein
Cheese and Sultana Blintzes	204	Traditional Cheese Blintzes	NFSS	Felicia Kahn
Cheese Borekas	196	Safta Fela's Borekas	AATF	Fela Levy
Chicken Barley Soup	220	Chicken and Barley Soup	MMCC	Barbara Solomon
Chicken Sambal	34	Fish Sambal	MMCC	Benjamin David
Chicken Soup	168	Simple Chicken Soup	TFGO	Lena Toropova
Chocolate 'Challah and Butter' Pudding	66	Chocolate 'Bread and Butter' Pudding	MMCC	Philip Carr (the late)
Chocolate Glaze (Chocolate Walnut Cake)	190	Chocolate Glaze	NFSS	Susie Clifford
Chocolate Sour Cream Kugelhopf	230	Kugelhopf	MMCC	May Stein (the late)
Chocolate Walnut Cake	190	Flourless Nutcake	TFGO	Yvonne Engelman
Chopped Herring Salad	23	Chopped Herring	MMCC	Melanie Knep
Chopped Liver	25	Chopped Liver	MMCC	Paula (MMCC) + Gary Horwitz
Cinnamon Brown Sugar Babke	72	Cinnamon Streusel Babke	NFSS	June Edelmuth
Cinnamon Doughnuts (Sufganiot)	156	Sufganiot	TFGO	Justine Cohen
Cinnamon Swirl Cake	69	Cinnamon Cake	TFGO	Varda Goodman
Cucumber Salad	229	Cucumber Salad	MMCC	Jacqui Israel (MMCC)
Double Chocolate Chiffon Cake	70	Chocolate Chiffon Cake	MMCC	Lyndi Adler
Fried Gefilte Fish	80	Gefilte Fish	TFGO	Ruth Eskin
Fried Meatballs (and Tomato Herb Salad)	151	Maria's Keftethes (Greek Meatballs)	TFGO	Antonia Haralambis
Ginger Date Slice	233	Neecey's Date Slice	MMCC	Janice Einfeld (the late)
Glazed Chicken Meatloaf	222	Aunty Raie's Meatloaf	MMCC	Raie (Fayn) Rosenberg (the late)

Recipe Name	Page	Previous Recipe Name	Book	Cook
Glazed Roman Lamb Shoulder	38	Roman Lamb	AATF	Myrna Rosen
Hamantashen, Three Ways (pastry)	158	Jam Ring Biscuits	AATF	Zoli 'John' Romer (the late)
Honey Peanut Tuiles	106	Honey Macadamia Wafers	MMCC	Barbara Solomon
Hungarian Beef Goulash	226	Veal Goulash	TFGO	Judy Kaye
Israeli Rice Pilaf	98	Israeli Rice Pilaf	AATF	Gloria Jacobson Pink
Israeli Salad with Farro and Chickpeas	154	Israeli Farro Salad	AATF	Amy Kritzer
Lamb and Date Tagine	87	Lamb Tagine with Dates	AATF	Ronit Robbaz
Lentil Rice (Majadara)	127	Majadara	MMCC	Anat Shechter
Matzo Balls	169	Balaclava Deli's Matzo Balls	TFGO	Lena Toropova
MMCC Eggplant Parmigiana	200	Buba's Eggplant	MMCC	Sharen Fink
Nokedli	228	Nokedli	MMCC	Elisabeth Varnai (the late)
'Not Fried' Lemon Garlic Chicken	33	Baked Mustard-Herb Chicken Legs	AATF	Debbie Glassman
Olive Oil Chocolate Mousse	46	Olive Oil Chocolate Mousse	AATF	Amos Roberts
Passionfruit Semifreddo	48	Passionfruit Ice Cream	AATF	Libby Skurnik
Peri-Peri Chicken Livers	27	Peri Peri Chicken Livers	MMCC	June Edelmuth
Persian Fish Pilau	28	Chicken Persian Pilau	MMCC	Molly Moses
Pickled Brisket with Honey Caramelized Onions	88	Sara's Pickled Brisket	MMCC	Sara (Fayn) Robenstone
Pickled Red Onion	56	Fish Tacos	AATF	Sharon Goldman
Pocket Pita Bread	63	Syrian Pita Bread	AATF	Huguette Ades
Poppyseed Beigli and Walnut Beigli	136	Beigli (Poppyseed and Walnut)	MMCC	Elisabeth Varnai (the late)
Pumpkin and Corn Salad with Tahina	124	Roasted Pumpkin and Sweetcorn Salad	AATF	Dov Sokoni
Rhubarb Strawberry Compote	215	Strawberry Rhubarb Cobbler	AATF	Dana Slatkin
Ricotta Cheesecake Slice	208	Hungarian Cheesecake	MMCC	Eva Grunstein (the late)
Roasted Apple Matzo Kugel	182	Matzo Kugel	TFGO	Roxanne Lambert Kozica
Roasted Carrot and Cauli Soup	218	Roasted Carrot and Fennel Soup	TFGO	Robyn Kaufman
Roasted Cherry Tomatoes (sauce) for Fish	170	Slow-roasted Tomato Sauce for Spaghetti	TFGO	Antonia Haralambis
Salmon Crumble	30	Salmon Crumble	TFGO	Lisa Breckler
Salmon Pastrami	54	Salmon Pastrami	TFGO	Lynn Niselow (MMCC)
Smashed Turmeric Potatoes	44	Roasted Turmeric Potatoes	MMCC	Molly Moses
Smashed Turmeric Potatoes	44	Smashed Potatoes	TFGO	Natalie Topper
Smoked Trout Fish Cakes	147	Fish Cakes	AATF	Lesley Cohen
Souhariki Biscotti	76	Souhariki	MMCC	Sharon Hendler (+ Vikki Biggs)
Sour Cherry Chocolate Brownies	234	Joan's on Third Chocolate Brownies	AATF	Joan McNamara
Spice-Crusted Whole Chicken	84	Chicken Everest	TFGO	Reuben (the late) + Charmaine Solomon
Spiced Barbecue Chicken with Green Hummus and Herb Salad	120	Middle Eastern Crunch Salad	TFGO	Georgia Samuel
Spiced Israeli Couscous with Eggplant	130	Ruby's Eggplant and Israeli Couscous Salad	TFGO	Yaron Finkelstein
The Essential Honey Cake	104	Gina's Hair-Raising Honey Cake	MMCC	Karen Gutman (+ Gina Swart)
Traybake Chicken with Zucchini and Fennel	173	Chicken with Olives and Capers	TFGO	Lisa Manoy
Turkish Spiced Snapper	118	Claypot Snapper	TFGO	Ata Gokyildirim
Yellow Rice	99	Yellow Rice	TFGO	Shereen Aaron

RECIPE ACKNOWLEDGEMENTS

Index

A

almonds
    Almond *Kifli* 238
    Almond Lemon
        Chiffon 186
    Coconut Almond
        Macaroons 193
apples
    Apple (Ashkenazi)
        Charoset 166
    Baked Apples 100
    Charoset Ice Cream
        Parfait 185
    Roasted Apple Cake 103
    Roasted Apple *Matzo*
        Kugel 182
Ashkenazi *Cholent* 42
Ashkenazi community 9
Ashkenazi food 9
Ata's Spice Blend 118
Avocado
    Avocado Dip 23
    Everyday Green Salad 44

B

babke
    Cinnamon Brown Sugar
        Babke 72
bagels
    Boiled Bagels 52
Baked Apples 100
Baked Cheesecake 210
barley
    Chicken Barley Soup 220

beans, broad
    Tel Aviv-Style Falafel 60
beans, kidney
    Ashkenazi *Cholent* 42
beans, white
    Ashkenazi *Cholent* 42
    Slow-Cooked
        Minestrone 115
beef
    Ashkenazi *Cholent* 42
    Fried Meatballs 151
    Hungarian Beef Goulash 226
    Kreplach (Jewish ravioli) 110
    Pickled Brisket with
        Honey Caramelised
        Onions 88
    Red Wine Brisket 176
    Rice and Beef Paprikash 225
    Rosh Hashanah Brisket 90
    Slow-Cooked Roast Beef 41
    Stuffed Cabbage Rolls 123
beigli
    Poppyseed *Beigli* 136
    Walnut *Beigli* 136
berries
    Rhubarb Strawberry
        Compote 215
    Thick Raspberry and
        Vanilla Jam Filling 159
biscotti and biscuits
    Almond *Kifli* 238
    biscuit dough 236
    Caraway Kakas 236
    Date Ginger Babas 236
    Honey Peanut Tuiles 106
    Souhariki Biscotti 76

blintzes
    Cheese and Sultana
        Blintzes 204
Boiled Bagels 52
borekas
    Cheese Borekas 196
Braised Red Cabbage 94
bread
    Boiled Bagels 52
    Challah 18
    Cinnamon Brown Sugar
        Babke 72
    Pangrattato 218
    Pocket Pita Bread 63
    Tangzhong starter 72
brisket 90
    cooking times 90, 176
    cutting 90
    Pickled Brisket with Honey
        Caramelised Onions 88
    Red Wine Brisket 176
    Rosh Hashanah Brisket 90
Broccoli Slaw 133
Brown Sugar Meringues 212
brownies
    Sour Cherry Chocolate
        Brownies 234
butter 13

C

cabbage
    Braised Red Cabbage 94
    Pickled Cabbage 61
    Spicy Cabbage Slaw 45
    Stuffed Cabbage Rolls 123

cake tins 13
cakes *see also* cheesecake
    Almond Lemon Chiffon 186
    Chocolate Sour Cream
       Kugelhopf 230
    Chocolate Walnut Cake 190
    Cinnamon Swirl Cake 69
    Double Chocolate Chiffon
       Cake 70
    Pear and Marmalade
       Cake 134
    Roasted Apple Cake 103
    The Essential Honey
       Cake 104
canola oil 14
Caraway Kakas 236
carrots
    Carrot *Tzimmes* 92
    Roasted Carrot and Cauli
       Soup 218
caster sugar 15
cauliflower
    Cauliflower and Sweet
       Potato Pilaf 128
    Roasted Carrot and Cauli
       Soup 218
Challah 18
    Chocolate '*Challah* and
       Butter' Pudding 66
Chalmers, Merelyn 6
Chanukah 143, 144
Charoset
    Apple (Ashkenazi)
       Charoset 166
    Charoset Ice Cream
       Parfait 185
    Date (Sephardi) *Charoset* 166
cheese
    Cheese and Spinach
       Borekas 196
    Cheese and Sultana
       Blintzes 204
    Cheese Borekas 196
    Ricotta Cheesecake Slice 208
    Sweet Cheese *Lokshen*
       Kugel 206
cheesecake
    Baked Cheesecake 210
    Ricotta Cheesecake Slice 208
cherries
    Sour Cherry Chocolate
       Brownies 234

chicken
    Chicken Barley Soup 220
    Chicken Sambal 34
    Chicken Schnitzel 150
    Chicken Soup 168
    Chicken Stock 218
    Glazed Chicken Meatloaf 222
    'Not Fried' Lemon Garlic
       Chicken 33
    Slow-Roasted, French-Style
       Roast Chicken 36
    Spice-Crusted Whole
       Chicken 84
    Spiced Barbecue Chicken
       with Green Hummus
       and Herb Salad 120
    Traybake Chicken with
       Zucchini and Fennel 173
chicken fat, rendered
   (*Schmaltz*) 14, 25
chicken livers
    Chopped Liver 25
    Peri-Peri Chicken Livers 27
chickpeas
    Green Hummus 120
    Israeli Salad with Farro
       and Chickpeas 154
    Pumpkin, Spinach and
       Chickpea Curry 116
    Slow-Cooked Minestrone 115
    Tel Aviv-Style Falafel 60
chocolate
    Chocolate Buttercream
       Icing 70
    Chocolate '*Challah* and
       Butter' Pudding 66
    Chocolate Glaze 190
    Chocolate *Rugelach* 140
    Chocolate Sour Cream
       Kugelhopf 230
    Chocolate Walnut Cake 190
    Double Chocolate Chiffon
       Cake 70
    melting 14
    Nut-Free Chocolate Torte 188
    Olive Oil Chocolate
       Mousse 46
    Sour Cherry Chocolate
       Brownies 234
Chopped Herring Salad 23
Chopped Liver 25
Cinnamon Brown Sugar Babke 72

Cinnamon Doughnuts
   (*Sufganiot*) 156
Cinnamon Sugar 13, 69
    coarse 156
Cinnamon Swirl Cake 69
Coconut Almond Macaroons 193
corn
    Pumpkin and Corn Salad
       with Tahina 124
couscous
    Spiced Israeli Couscous
       with Eggplant 130
cream cheese
    Baked Cheesecake 210
    Cheese and Sultana
       Blintzes 204
    Cream Cheese Shallot
       Shmear 57
    Sweet Cheese *Lokshen*
       Kugel 206
Crepe Batter 204
crumble
    Roasted Plum Crumble 64
Cucumber Salad 229
curry
    Pumpkin, Spinach and
       Chickpea Curry 116

D

dairy free
    Almond Lemon Chiffon 186
    Chocolate Walnut Cake 190
    Cinnamon Swirl Cake 69
    Olive Oil Chocolate
       Mousse 46
    Passionfruit Semifreddo 48
    Pear and Marmalade
       Cake 134
    Souhariki Biscotti 76
dates
    Date Ginger Babas 236
    Date (Sephardi) *Charoset* 166
    Ginger Date Slice 233
    Lamb and Date Tagine 87
desserts *see also* cakes
    Baked Apples 100
    Brown Sugar Meringues 212
    Charoset Ice Cream
       Parfait 185
    Chocolate '*Challah* and Butter'
       Pudding 66

Nut-Free Chocolate
    Torte 188
Olive Oil Chocolate
    Mousse 46
Passionfruit Semifreddo 48
Roasted Apple *Matzo*
    Kugel 182
Roasted Plum Crumble 64
Sweet Cheese *Lokshen*
    Kugel 206
dip *see also shmears*
    Avocado Dip 23
Double Chocolate Chiffon
    Cake 70
dressing
    Everyday Green Salad, for 44
    Israeli Salad with Farro and
        Chickpeas, for 154
    Spicy Cabbage Slaw, for 45

E

eggplant
    MMCC Eggplant
        Parmigiana 200
    Spiced Israeli Couscous
        with Eggplant 130
eggs 14
    Egg and Onion 24
    raw eggs, using 14
electric mixers 13
Erev Shabbat 17
Eskin, Natanya 7
Everyday Green Salad 44

F

falafel
    Tel Aviv-Style Falafel 60
farro
    Israeli Salad with Farro
        and Chickpeas 154
fennel
    Traybake Chicken with
        Zucchini and Fennel 173
fish
    Chopped Herring Salad 23
    Fish with Roasted Cherry
        Tomatoes 170
    Fried *Gefilte* Fish 80
    Maple Soy Salmon 83
    Persian Fish Pilau 28

Salmon Crumble 30
Salmon Pastrami 54
Salmon with Tahina and
    Herbs 198
Smoked Trout Fish Cakes 147
Tuna Salad *Shmear* 57
Turkish Spiced Snapper 118
flour
    bread flour 14
    plain flour 14
    self-raising flour 14
French shallots 15
Fried *Gefilte* Fish 80
Fried Meatballs 151

G

garlic
    'Not Fried' Lemon Garlic
        Chicken 33
ginger
    Date Ginger Babas 236
    Ginger Date Slice 233
Glazed Chicken Meatloaf 222
Glazed Roman Lamb
    Shoulder 38
gluten free
    Almond Lemon Chiffon 186
    Baked Apples 100
    Chocolate Walnut Cake 190
    Nut-Free Chocolate Torte 188
Goldberg, Lisa 6
grapeseed oil 14
gratin
    Potato Gratin 203
Greek-Style, Slow-Cooked
    Lamb 174
gribenes 15

H

Hafrashat blessing 19
Haggadah 163, 164
Hamantashen 158
    Nutella and Halva Filling 159
    'Stuffed Monkey' Filling 159
    Thick Raspberry and Vanilla
        Jam Filling 159
herbs 14
    Herb Salad and dressing 120
    Salmon with Tahina and
        Herbs 198

Slow-Roasted, French-Style
    Roast Chicken 36
Tomato Herb Salad 153
herring
    Chopped Herring Salad 23
honey 79
    Carrot *Tzimmes* 92
    Honey Peanut Tuiles 106
    Pickled Brisket with
        Honey Caramelised
        Onions 88
    The Essential Honey
        Cake 104
hospitality 17
hummus
    Green Hummus 120
Hungarian Beef Goulash 226
Hungarian dumplings (*Nokedli*)
    228

I

iced desserts
    Charoset Ice Cream
        Parfait 185
    Passionfruit Semifreddo 48
icing
    Chocolate Buttercream
        Icing 70
    Chocolate Glaze 190
    Lemon Icing 186
icing sugar mixture 15
Israeli Rice Pilaf 98
Israeli Salad with Farro and
    Chickpeas 154

J

Jewish communities 9
Jewish food, classifications 9

K

kakas
    Caraway Kakas 236
kashrut dietary laws 13
kifli
    Almond *Kifli* 238
kosher, keeping 13
    dietary requirements,
        website 13
Kreplach (Jewish ravioli) 110

L

lamb
    Glazed Roman Lamb Shoulder 38
    Greek-Style, Slow-Cooked Lamb 174
    Lamb and Date Tagine 87
latkes
    Potato Latkes 144
Leek and Mushroom *Matzo* Brei 180
lemons
    Almond Lemon Chiffon 186
    Lemon Icing 186
    lemon juice 14
    'Not Fried' Lemon Garlic Chicken 33
Lentil Rice (*Majadara*) 127
lettuce
    Everyday Green Salad 44
lining tins or trays 13
livers
    Chopped Liver 25
    Peri-Peri Chicken Livers 27

M

ma nishtana 163
macaroons
    Coconut Almond Macaroons 193
Majadara (Lentil Rice) 127
Maple Soy Salmon 83
marmalade
    Pear and Marmalade Cake 134
matzo 10, 163, 166, 169
    Matzo Balls 169
    Matzo Brei 180
    Roasted Apple *Matzo* Kugel 182
Matzo Brei
    Basic *Matzo* Brei 180
    Leek and Mushroom *Matzo* Brei 180
measurements and conversions 13
meatballs
    Fried Meatballs 151
meatloaf
    Glazed Chicken Meatloaf 222

meringues
    Brown Sugar Meringues 212
Minestrone, Slow-Cooked 115
mitzvah (good deed) 19, 109, 130
mitzvot commandments 17
Mizrachi community 9
MMCC Eggplant Parmigiana 200
MMCC Tomato Sauce 200
mushrooms
    Leek and Mushroom *Matzo* Brei 180

N

Nokedli 228
'Not Fried' Lemon Garlic Chicken 33
Nut-Free Chocolate Torte 188
nuts
    Almond *Kifli* 238
    Almond Lemon Chiffon 186
    Chocolate Walnut Cake 190
    Coconut Almond Macaroons 193
    Honey Peanut Tuiles 106
    Walnut *Beigli* 136

O

oil
    canola oil 14
    extra virgin olive oil 14
    grapeseed oil 14
    light olive oil 14
    unflavoured 14
olive oil 14
Olive Oil Chocolate Mousse 46
onions
    Pickled Brisket with Honey Caramelised Onions 88
    Pickled Red Onion 56
ovens and oven cooking temperatures 13

P

Pangrattato 218
paprika
    Hungarian Beef Goulash 226
    Rice and Beef Paprikash 225

parfait
    Charoset Ice Cream Parfait 185
parmigiana
    MMCC Eggplant Parmigiana 200
Passionfruit Semifreddo 48
Passover (*Pesach*) 163–4, 182
pastries
    Cheese and Spinach Borekas 196
    Cheese Borekas 196
    Chocolate *Rugelach* 140
    Hamantashen Three Ways 158–9
    Poppyseed *Beigli* 136
    Walnut *Beigli* 136
pastry
    beigli, for 136
    borekas, for 196
    hamantashen, for 158
    Ricotta Cheesecake Slice, for 208
    rugelach, for 140
peanuts
    Honey Peanut Tuiles 106
Pear and Marmalade Cake 134
pepper 15
Peri-Peri Chicken Livers 27
Persian Fish Pilau 28
Pesach (Passover) 163–4, 182
    seder dinner 163, 164
Pickled Brisket with Honey Caramelised Onions 88
Pickled Cabbage 61
Pickled Red Onion 56
pickles
    Pickled Cabbage 61
    Pickled Red Onion 56
pilaf
    Cauliflower and Sweet Potato Pilaf 128
    Israeli Rice Pilaf 98
pilau
    Persian Fish Pilau 28
pita bread
    Pocket Pita Bread 63
plums
    Roasted Plum Crumble 64
Pocket Pita Bread 63
Poppyseed *Beigli* 136
Potato Kugel 95

potatoes
    Potato Gratin 203
    Potato Kugel 95
    Potato Latkes 144
    Potato *Ulnyik* 178
    Smashed Turmeric Potatoes 44
puddings
    Chocolate '*Challah* and Butter' Pudding 66
    Roasted Apple *Matzo* Kugel 182
pumpkin
    Pumpkin and Corn Salad with Tahina 124
    Pumpkin, Spinach and Chickpea Curry 116
Purim 143, 158

R

red onions
    Pickled Red Onion 56
Red Wine Brisket 176
Rhubarb Strawberry Compote 215
rice
    Cauliflower and Sweet Potato Pilaf 128
    Israeli Rice Pilaf 98
    Lentil Rice (*Majadara*) 127
    Persian Fish Pilau 28
    Rice and Beef Paprikash 225
    Yellow Rice 99
ricotta
    Ricotta Cheesecake Slice 208
    Sweet Cheese *Lokshen* Kugel 206
Roasted Apple Cake 103
Roasted Plum Crumble 64
Rosh Hashanah 10, 79, 80
Rosh Hashanah Brisket 90
rugelach
    Chocolate *Rugelach* 140

S

salads
    Broccoli Slaw 133
    Chopped Herring Salad 23
    Cucumber Salad 229
    Everyday Green Salad 44
    Herb Salad and dressing 120
    Israeli Salad with Farro and Chickpeas 154
    Pumpkin and Corn Salad with Tahina 124
    Spiced Israeli Couscous with Eggplant 130
    Spicy Cabbage Slaw 45
    Tomato Herb Salad 153
salmon
    Maple Soy Salmon 83
    Salmon Crumble 30
    Salmon Pastrami 54
    Salmon with Tahina and Herbs 198
salt 15
sambal
    Chicken Sambal 34
    Sambal Sauce 34
sauces
    MMCC Tomato Sauce 200
    Sambal Sauce 34
    Tahina Sauce 61, 124, 153
    Tahina Yoghurt Sauce 198
schmaltz 14
schnitzel
    Chicken Schnitzel 150
semifreddo
    Passionfruit Semifreddo 48
Sephardi community 9, 84
    Baghdadi-Indian 28
Sephardi food 9, 34, 99
'seven species of fruits' 154
Shabbat 17
    cooking on, laws about 17, 42
    Shabbat dinner 17
    Shabbat lunch 17
shallots 15
    Cream Cheese Shallot *Shmear* 57
    French shallots 15
Shavuot 195
Shiva 217
shmears 23
    Avocado Dip 23
    Chopped Liver 25
    Cream Cheese Shallot *Shmear* 57
    Egg and Onion 24
    Tuna Salad *Shmear* 57
shofar (ram's horn) 79

slaw
    Broccoli Slaw 133
    Spicy Cabbage Slaw 45
slices
    Ginger Date Slice 233
    Sour Cherry Chocolate Brownies 234
Slow-Cooked Minestrone 115
Slow-Cooked Roast Beef 41
Slow-Roasted, French-Style Roast Chicken 36
slow-roasts
    Glazed Roman Lamb Shoulder 38
    Greek-Style, Slow-Cooked Lamb 174
    Slow-Cooked Roast Beef 41
    Slow-Roasted, French-Style Roast Chicken 36
Smashed Turmeric Potatoes 44
Smoked Trout Fish Cakes 147
snapper
    Turkish Spiced Snapper 118
Souhariki Biscotti 76
soups
    Chicken Barley Soup 220
    Chicken Soup 168
    Chicken Stock 218
    Roasted Carrot and Cauli Soup 218
    Slow-Cooked Minestrone 115
Sour Cherry Chocolate Brownies 234
sour cream
    Chocolate Sour Cream Kugelhopf 230
Spice-Crusted Whole Chicken 84
Spiced Barbecue Chicken with Green Hummus and Herb Salad 120
Spiced Israeli Couscous with Eggplant 130
spices
    Ata's Spice Blend 118
    Spice-Crusted Whole Chicken, paste for 84
    Za'atar 154
Spicy Cabbage Slaw 45

spinach
> Cheese and Spinach Borekas 196
> Pumpkin, Spinach and Chickpea Curry 116

strawberries
> Rhubarb Strawberry Compote 215

Stuffed Cabbage Rolls 123
stuffed foods 109
Sufganiot (Cinnamon Doughnuts) 156
sugar
> caster sugar 15
> icing sugar mixture 15
> white (granulated) sugar 15

sukkah 109
Sukkot 109
sultanas
> Baked Apples 100
> Cheese and Sultana *Blintzes* 204

Sunday brunch 51
Sweet Cheese *Lokshen* Kugel 206
sweet potato
> Cauliflower and Sweet Potato Pilaf 128

T

tagine
> Lamb and Date Tagine 87

Tahina Sauce 61, 124, 153
> Tahina Yoghurt Sauce 198

Tangzhong starter 72
Tel Aviv-Style Falafel 60
Ten Commandments 195
The Essential Honey Cake 104
tomatoes
> Fish with Roasted Cherry Tomatoes 170
> MMCC Eggplant Parmigiana 200
> MMCC Tomato Sauce 200
> Stuffed Cabbage Rolls 123
> Tomato Herb Salad 153

Torah 195
torte
> Nut-Free Chocolate Torte 188

Traybake Chicken with Zucchini and Fennel 173

trout
> Smoked Trout Fish Cakes 147

Tu Bishvat 143, 154
tuiles
> Honey Peanut Tuiles 106

Tuna Salad *Shmear* 57
Turkish Spiced Snapper 118
turmeric
> Smashed Turmeric Potatoes 44
> Yellow Rice 99

V

vegan
> Lentil Rice *(Majadara)* 127
> Pumpkin, Spinach and Chickpea Curry 116

W

walnuts
> Chocolate Walnut Cake 190
> Walnut *Beigli* 136

website
> mondaymorningcookingclub.com.au 13

white (granulated) sugar 15

Y

yeast 15
Yellow Rice 99
Yoghurt
> Yoghurt Cream 215
> Tahina Yoghurt Sauce 198

Yom Kippur (Day of Atonement) 79

Z

Za'atar 154
zucchini
> Traybake Chicken with Zucchini and Fennel 173

Thanks

Neverending thanks to our wonderful growing families for even more love and encouragement, and for accepting that we just had to do one more book and they had to try just one more slow-cooked brisket.

Biggest hugs to our extended sisterhood Jacqui Israel, Lauren Fink, Lynn Niselow and Paula Horwitz (and her amazing Field to Fork butcher), who we miss in the kitchen but know they are supporting us from the sidelines.

The hugest appreciation to Rachel Bundang Quintana behind the scenes, helping us every day in the kitchen and on location. Nothing was ever too much trouble and we couldn't have done any of it without you.

Since our early days, it has been a dream of ours to work with Julie Gibbs, Australia's pre-eminent cookbook publisher. Thank you Julie for giving us very long apron strings while we did our usual testing, tasting and tinkering. What a joy it has been to work with you over many cups of tea and perhaps too many slices of cake.

An MMCC book would not be an MMCC book without the incredible Alan Benson. The brother in our sisterhood. Supremely professional, kind, funny and absolutely so bloody good at his job.

We loved working with fabulous food stylist Justine Poole for the first time. It was such a pleasure. Thank you also to Amber de Florio for stepping in for the first couple of days, getting us started on the road to a gorgeous book.

To our wonderful production team, editor Pru Engel, designer Hannah Schubert and project manager Katrina O'Brien, thank you for helping to create a beautiful book that we are so incredibly proud of.

Continuing thanks to our solicitors Arnold Bloch Leibler, accountants MBP Advisory, and accountant Christopher Rutter of Dakota Corporation, for doing all the things needed to run a business that we still have no idea how to do. And for doing it all pro bono.

More thanks to Mandy Meltz, who happens to be Lisa's *machatenista*, for her guidance on all things Jewish. To Michael Rantissi for sharing not only his recipes, but his heart and soul.

Monday Morning Cooking Club is, and has always been, a not-for-profit company and 100 per cent of all our profits from the sales of our books go to various charities across Australia. Visit mondaymorningcookingclub.com.au for a comprehensive list.

Warmest thanks to those of you who came before us and created a Jewish kitchen, often against the odds. Your heartfelt and emotional stories, your can't-live-without recipes and your deep connection to Jewish heritage has created the foundation for this book and ultimately our project, which tells the story of our community.

We are now ready to welcome the next generation into our year of Jewish cooking.

A YEAR OF JEWISH COOKING:
RECIPES WE CAN'T LIVE WITHOUT
First published in Australia in 2026 by
Simon & Schuster (Australia) Pty Limited
Level 4, 32 York St, Sydney NSW 2000

10 9 8 7 6 5 4 3 2 1

New York Amsterdam/Antwerp London Toronto Sydney/Melbourne New Delhi
Visit our website at www.simonandschuster.com.au

For more than 100 years, Simon & Schuster has championed authors and the stories they create. By respecting the copyright of an author's intellectual property, you enable Simon & Schuster and the author to continue publishing exceptional books for years to come. We thank you for supporting the author's copyright by purchasing an authorised edition of this book.

No amount of this book may be reproduced or stored in any format, nor may it be uploaded to any website, database, language-learning model, or other repository, retrieval, or artificial intelligence system without express permission. All rights reserved. Inquiries may be directed to Simon & Schuster, 1230 Avenue of the Americas, New York, NY 10020 or permissions@simonandschuster.com.

Text © Lisa Goldberg, Merelyn Chalmers, Natanya Eskin 2026
Photography © Alan Benson 2026

All rights reserved. No part of this publication may be reproduced, stored in a retrieval system, or transmitted in any form or by any means, electronic, mechanical, photocopying, recording or otherwise, without prior permission of the publisher.

A catalogue record for this book is available from the National Library of Australia

 A catalogue record for this book is available from the National Library of Australia

ISBN: 9781761426759

Designer: Hannah Schubert
Photographer: Alan Benson
Stylists: Justine Poole and Amber de Florio
Editor: Pru Engel
Project manager: Katrina O'Brien
Proofreader: Samantha Jones

Printed and bound in China by RR Donnelley

 The paper this book is printed on is from FSC® certified forests and other controlled sources. FSC® promotes environmentally responsible, socially beneficial and economically viable management of the world's forests.